WINGS OVER WATER

A chronicle of the flying boats and amphibians of the twentieth century

WINGS OVER WATER

A chronicle of the flying boats and amphibians of the twentieth century

David Oliver

THE LUXURY
OF THE EMPIRE
FLYING-BOAT

CHARTWELL
BOOKS, INC.

Picture credits

Author: 6, 7, 8, 12, 18, 19, 20, 23, 24, 25, 34 (left), 40 (center left), 41 (right), 44 (left), 45 (below right), 54 (right), 61, 64 (left), 66 (right), 67 (top right), 69 (left), 71 (right), 72 (left), 80, 81 (above), 83 (right), 87, 88, 89 (above), 90, 91, 95, 96, 97 (left), 100 (below), 101 (above left), 102 (above), 103, 105, 106, 108, 110 (left), 111, 112, 113, 114, 117 (left), 120, 121, 122 (above); **Francois Prins:** 9, 11, 13 (top/above), 26 (top), 34 (below right), 39 (center left/above), 40 (top), 41 (top), 42 (top right), 43 (right/center right/top right), 47 (top), 49 (top), 53 (above), 57 (top right), 66 (below left), 69 (right), 73 (top right), 74, 75, 79 (above/top), 92, 97 (below), 99 (right), 100 (above/left), 102 (above); **Terry Gwynn-Jones Collection:** 13 (left), 14, 51 (left); **RNZAF:** 15, 71 (below), 87 (top); **Royal Aeronautical Society:** 17, 50 (above), 58, 59, 79, 98; **Ken Ellis Collection:** 21, 26 (above), 27, 28, 37 (above), 39 (top/center right), 73 (right), 101 (below); **Dornier:** 29, 30, 31, 33, 63; **John Bachelor:** 32 (above), 40, 46, 72; **Popperfoto:** 32 (left), 42 (left), 81 (left); **Cobham:** 43 (left); **Frederick Lert:** 49 (above/below left); **Pan Am Historical Foundation:** 50 (below), 51 (top), 52 (above left/left), 56 (above), 57 (above left), 59 (top left); **Barry Wheeler:** 53, 59, 95 (left), 97 (below); **John Wegg:** 54, 55 (below/left), 58 (below); **Peter J Bish:** 60; **Konstantin Udalov:** 65, 89 (top/above), 122 (right), 125 (right); **Brett Freeman:** 67 (top), 68 (below left), 69 (above), 70 (above/below), 107 (above); **P R March:** 68 (right); **QANTAS:** 70 (below), 99 (left); **The Glenn L Martin Aviation Museum:** 76, 85 (above), 86 (left); **Lockheed Martin:** 77, 84 (center/bottom), 85 (above left/below); **Warren Thompson:** 82; **Paul Duffy:** 84 (top), 119; **Keith Sissons:** 102 (below); **Frank B Mormillo:** 104, 110 (above); **Robert Rudhall/FP:** 109 (left); **Warrior:** 115, 124 (left), 125 (above); **Canadair:** 115 (right/below right), 116; **Ross:** 123 (above left); **Nauticair:** 124 (below), 125; **AVPRO UK:** 126, 127; **MAP:** 34 (top), 35 (right), 59, 67; **Vintage Magazine Archive:** 3, 40, 44, 93; **ET Archive:** 16; **Musée Air France [by artist Albert Brenet]:** 35 (top)

The publisher would like to thank all of the individuals and companies for contributing illustrative material for this book.

While every effort has been made to ensure that all credits are listed, the Publisher apologizes for any omissions.

A QUINTET BOOK

Published by Chartwell Books
A Division of Book Sales, Inc.
114, Northfield Avenue,
Edison, New Jersey 08837

This edition produced for sale in the U.S.A.,
its territories and dependencies only.

ISBN 0-7858-1043-9

This book was designed and produced by
Quintet Publishing Limited
6 Blundell Street
London N7 9BH

Creative Director: Richard Dewing
Art Director: Simon Daley
Designer: James Lawrence
Project Editor: Debbie Foy

Typeset in Great Britain by
Central Southern Typesetters, Eastbourne
Manufactured in China by Regent Publishing Services Ltd.
Printed in Singapore by Star Standard Industries (PTE) Ltd.

CONTENTS

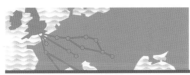

INTRODUCTION

It is exactly thirty years ago that I landed on the calm, blue waters of Catalina Island's Avalon Bay lying some 50 miles off the coast of southern California, in a 30-year-old Grumman amphibian, the Goose. As the veteran flying boat settled in a flurry of blue green water that covered the windows for a few seconds, it seemed that I had experienced the last of a dying breed of flight. I had flown from London to Los Angeles a few days earlier on one of Pan Am's first "Jumbo Jets" and the old six-seater Goose, which still flew hourly shuttles for tourists between Long Beach Harbor and Catalina, seemed to have no relevance to international air travel in the modern world.

However, it was small amphibious flying boats that flew the first international passenger services in the United States and in Europe, and it was the commercial flying boat that opened up the world to air travel. Their development was inspired by two great airlines that were established in the 1920s whose remarkable route networks covered most of the world by the end of the 1930s—Imperial Airways and Pan American Airways Inc. The British airline opened up its "Empire" routes to Africa, India, and Hong Kong, while Pan Am pioneered the Pacific, Atlantic, and South American routes.

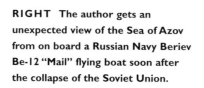

RIGHT The author gets an unexpected view of the Sea of Azov from on board a Russian Navy Beriev Be-12 "Mail" flying boat soon after the collapse of the Soviet Union.

The high-tech flying boats designed for these airlines were the most advanced commercial aircraft flying by the eve of World War Two, carrying up to 50 passengers in extreme luxury over thousands of miles at speeds of more than 200 miles an hour—faster than many fighters of the day.

Although World War Two halted commercial flying boat development, military derivatives of the Empire Boats and Pan Am Clippers were built in their thousands and saw extensive service with all the combatants in all theaters of war as maritime reconnaissance bombers, air-sea rescue aircraft, and long-range transports.

Despite their wartime success, the end of hostilities almost signaled the end of the flying boat which had by then been overtaken by the rapid development of land planes which could now operate from airfields built largely by the military in nearly every country on the globe.

LEFT At the San Pedro seaplane terminal at Long Beach, California is the Air Catalina Grumman Goose in which the author first experienced the unique sensation of landing and taking off in an aircraft from water.

Commercial aviation soon forsook the flying boat apart from on some remote routes between Pacific islands, in the Caribbean, Alaska, and South America. Military flying boats proved to be more expensive to develop and operate than equivalent land planes and the only remaining preserve of the flying boat in the 1950s and 1960s seemed to be bush flyers and sportsmen who used thousands of small amphibians and light aircraft fitted with floats for fishing trips and cargo flights to remote rivers and lakes mainly in North America.

However, it was one of nature's most destructive elements— fire, that would virtually save the large flying boat from extinction. The growing cost of devastating forest fires in Canada prompted its government to sponsor the development of a dedicated firefighting aircraft, and the most suitable design for this specialized role turned out to be a large flying boat. First built in the 1970s, nearly 200 Canadair CL-215 and 415 amphibians have been produced and are continuing to be produced. The success of the Canadair has led the lives of older ex-military flying boats to be extended well beyond their design life by being modified as aerial firefighters, and new flying boats have been developed by several countries to compete with the Canadian amphibian. Against all the odds the type currently enjoys a much healthier state than at any time in the last 50 years and looks set to develop and flourish in the future.

The following chapters will see the rise and fall, and rise again of the flying boat which has always had unique capabilities that no other flying machine can match. From the very birth of manned flight to its development as a warplane in World War One, a vital tool for world explorers in the 1920s, the symbol of luxurious and sophisticated travel in the 1930s, the U-boat killer of World War Two, and its postwar decline, to its increasingly important environmental role in the near and distant future. Long live the flying boat.

David Oliver

TOP RIGHT The view of a British yacht on the River Medway seen over the pilot's shoulder while water-taxiing a Lake Buccaneer amphibian during the author's first lesson in a flying boat.

RIGHT The Grumman Goose takes to the water in Seal Cove, Prince Rupert, British Columbia, Canada where the 50-year-old amphibian still operates scheduled service from Queen Charlotte Islands.

O ver the centuries, ancient mariners have dreamt of being lifted into the air to fly on the invisible air currents used by the sea birds that follow their craft across the oceans. It seemed a logical solution to fit boats with ever larger sails or wings enabling them to take off and soar over the water— the best of both worlds.

LEFT The Sopwith Baby, a more powerful development of the Schneider-winning Tabloid, was the RNAS (Royal Naval Air Service's) first fighter scout when it entered service in 1916.

ABOVE Savoia-Type F FBA training and observation flying boats built during World War One were used for the first air passenger services in Europe from Zurichhorn in 1918.

HANSA-BRANDENBURG CC

Imperial Austro-German single-seat flying boat fighter
flown by Austro-Hungarian Navy "ace" Gottfried Banfield
was designed by Ernst Heinkel who established his own
company in 1922.

STATISTICS

Wingspan	30ft 6in	
Length	25ft 3in	
Height	11ft 8in	
Weight	Empty 1,764lb	Loaded 2,381lb
Engines	180hp Hiero piston engine	
Max speed	112mph	
Cruise speed	103mph	
Range	300 miles	
Armament	8mm Schwarzlose machine gun	

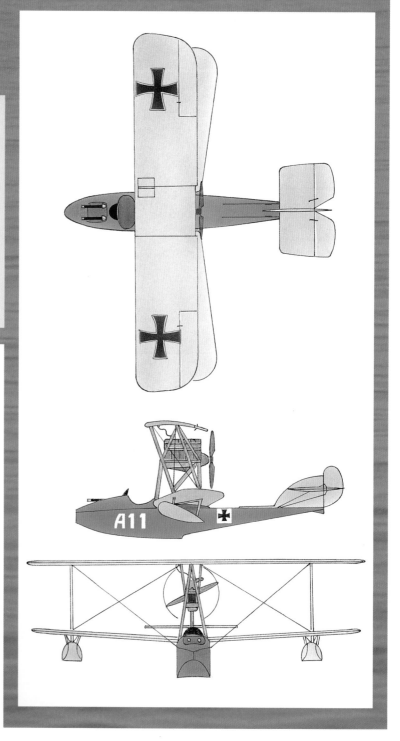

THE PIONEERS

Many early aviation pioneers experimented with both bizarre and
ingenious designs for the first flying boat. One who was ahead of
his time was the sixteenth-century Jesuit priest Francesco de
Lana-Terzi who designed a boat-carriage which would be lifted
into the air by four large copper globes from which all the air had
been extracted by an air pump. The globes would then be lighter
than the air surrounding them and they would float upward,
lifting the boat off the water. It might have worked but he decided
not to build his "flying boat" in case it fell into the wrong hands
and was used to drop boiling oil or flaming arrows onto ships and
soldiers in time of war.

Man finally took to the air aboard hot-air and gas-filled
balloons and airships, but the dream of a flying boat persisted into
the twentieth century. It was the invention of the internal
combustion engine that proved to be the spur for successful
heavier-than-air flight. However, a hybrid flying boat came close

to beating the Wright brothers in achieving the first man-carrying, powered, sustained flight.

American mathematician Samuel Pierpoint Langley had launched a number of steam-engine-powered unmanned heavier-than-air craft from a houseboat moored on the Potomac River in 1893, and was awarded $50,000 by the US government to construct a full-size manned version. By August 1903 Langley had flown a quarter-scale model which became the first craft powered by a petroleum engine to achieve sustained flight. His full-size aircraft, named *Aerodrome*, powered by a 52hp Manly-Balzer petroleum engine made an unsuccessful flight in October 1903 with a Charles M Manly at the controls. Manly made another attempt on October 9 but, as before, the *Aerodrome* dropped into the river. Three weeks later the Wright brothers successfully flew their *Flyer* into the history books and Langley's efforts were largely forgotten.

The race to build a practical heavier-than-air flying boat now moved to Europe. Wealthy automobile accessory manufacturer and aviation pioneer Louis Blériot took up the challenge. Never having flown before, Blériot began to design and fly a variety of weird and wonderful craft, some of which had been developed to take off and land on water. One of these was the ungainly Blériot IV seaplane which featured an elliptical tail and made some unsuccessful attempts to take off from Lac d'Enghien in 1906. Three years later Blériot designed his Type XI, a monoplane landplane which was destined to become one of the decade's most successful aircraft.

It fell to another Frenchman, Henri Fabre, to make the first successful powered take-off from water on March 28, 1910. His fragile floatplane, which resembled a stick-insect, was powered by a Gnome-pusher engine and named *Hydravion*. It took off from Le Méde harbor at Martigues near Marseilles. The aircraft was destroyed a year later when it crashed into Monaco harbor while being flown by Jean Becue, but by that time the first successful take-off and landing from water had been accomplished—in California.

TOP RIGHT Henri Fabre (1882–1984) seen by the Gnome-pusher engine of his *Hydravion* which made the first powered flight from water on March 28, 1910 at La Méde harbor in the south of France.

RIGHT Fabre's *Hydravion* in Monaco harbor in March 1911, which the pilot, Jean Becue (seen here), crashed later the same day. Becue was rescued but the historic floatplane was destroyed.

Glen H Curtiss had gained fame in the United States racing motorcycles which he built himself. Inspired by the Wright brothers, Curtiss became the first American to follow them when he flew his *June Bug* for the first time over a distance of 1,266 feet on June 20, 1908. On July 4, Curtiss flew his aircraft over a measured course to win the Scientific America trophy worth $2,500. Curtiss's success led to rivalry between him and the Wright brothers and in March 1909, when he formed a company to produce aircraft and aircraft engines, the Wright brothers issued a writ alleging that Curtiss was using their patents and designs without paying royalties.

However, in the meantime Curtiss had left for Europe where his dramatic victory in the Gordon Bennett Cup race at Rheims led to overwhelming demand for his aircraft and engines. In 1910, Curtiss modified the winning *Rheims Flyer* with a large center float and two smaller floats under each wing to produce the A-1 Hydroaeroplane. In January 1911, Glen Curtiss made the first successful take-off, landing, water-taxi, and another take-off by a powered aircraft in San Diego harbor. Six months later a Curtiss A-1 became the US Navy's very first aircraft. The single-seat A-1 was later fitted with retractable wheels to become the first amphibian and by 1913 Curtiss had sold more than 40 A-1s to wealthy amateur aviators as well as to the navies of Russia, Germany, and Japan.

In 1912, brothers Allen and Malcolm Loughead formed the Alco Hydro-Aeroplane Company in San Francisco, California and produced the Model G, a single-engine amphibian which could carry two people. Although it attracted no orders, Alco later built a small number of Curtiss HS-2L flying boats under license and constructed a 10-seat F-1 flying boat—designed by a young John K Northrop—but this was another commercial failure. In 1921, the company went bankrupt but was re-formed five years later as the Lockheed Aircraft Company.

Meanwhile, in an effort to promote European development of the seaplane, a French industrialist and entrepreneur, M Jacques Schneider, offered a trophy for an international maritime aviation competition. Entrants sponsored by their national aero clubs had

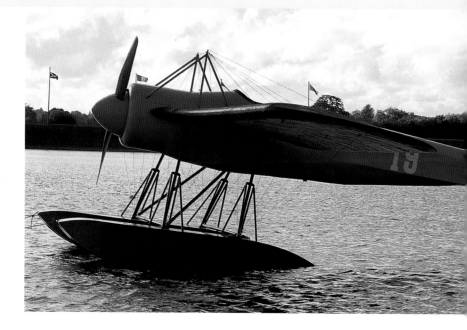

ABOVE The first Schneider Trophy contest held in Monaco for seaplanes was won by Frenchman Maurice Prévost flying a 160hp Gnome-powered Deperdussin floatplane, in April 1913.

to complete five laps of a 30-nautical-mile triangular closed circuit; the one putting up the fastest time would win the trophy. The winner's national aero club would then host the next contest. Held at Monaco on April 16, 1913, the first contest was won by Frenchman Maurice Prévost flying a 160hp Gnome-powered Deperdussin floatplane at an average speed of 45.75mph. This low speed was due to the fact that Prévost touched down before the finishing line and had to fly a complete extra lap. Despite this, the winning aircraft's performance had impressed the Royal Navy, which ordered a Deperdussin "flying boat," the service's first aircraft, a few days later. The service also ordered its first real flying boat, the British Sopwith Bat-Boat, three of which were delivered between June 1913 and February 1914.

FLYING BOATS COME OF AGE

In the months leading up to the outbreak of World War One, flying boats were coming of age and beginning to make their mark in both the growing military and civil sectors of aviation. On January 21, 1914 the world's first regular passenger air service, flown between Tampa and St Petersburg, Florida was inaugurated using a Benoist flying boat carrying a single passenger. The second Schneider contest was held at Monaco on April 20 with entries from Great Britain, France, Germany,

Switzerland, and America. In the event, only two competitors completed the course, the fastest of which was a diminutive British Sopwith Tabloid floatplane flown by Howard "Picky" Pixton at an average speed of 86.6mph.

Five days later, flying boats went to war for the first time. Five US Navy Curtiss ABs had been deployed to Veracruz in Mexico aboard the battleship USS *Mississippi* and the cruiser USS *Birmingham* to assist in military operations during the Mexican crisis. On April 25, Lt Bellinger took off in AB-3 to search for mines in Veracruz harbor. Although some of the flying boats were hit by rifle fire, none of the aircraft were lost. Curtiss flying boats continued to make the headlines over the next few weeks when the flying boat *Sunfish* made the first passenger flight in Canada from Toronto to Hamilton and back on May 15.

However, despite his success in producing the world's most advanced flying boats, Curtiss was still locked in litigation with the Wright brothers. Wilbur Wright had died in May, 1912 at the age of 45, with his brother claiming that the stress of the patent case had hastened his death. In January 1914, Orville Wright seemed to have won his case when a US Circuit Court of Appeals judgement upheld the Wright brothers' claim to be the "true pioneers of the practical art of flying heavier-than-air machines."

LEFT The Benoist flying boat which flew the world's first scheduled commercial passenger service from St Petersburg to Tampa in Florida in January 1914.

TOP The first British flying boat was the Sopwith Bat-Boat, which featured a polished mahogany hull. Three of them were ordered by the Admiralty in 1913.

ABOVE The second Schneider Trophy contest at Monaco was won by the British pilot Howard "Picky" Pixton, pictured here standing on the float, flying a Sopwith Tabloid at an average speed of 86.6mph on April 20, 1914.

Ironically, Curtiss had been awarded the Smithsonian Institution's Langley Medal in 1913 for outstanding work in the development of the flying boat. Not only had he won its award, but Curtiss also persuaded the Institution to rebuild Langley's unsuccessful flying boat, the *Aerodrome*, to prove that it had been a viable flying machine even before the Wright brothers flew. The *Aerodrome* was brought out of storage and transported to the Curtiss factory at Hammondsport in New York state. Unknown to the Smithsonian, which had contributed $2,000 to the project, Curtiss secretly modified the Langley flying boat by changing its center of gravity and the camber of the wings, and fitting an 80hp Curtiss engine. On May 28, 1914 Glen Curtiss successfully flew the *Buzzard*, as it was now known, from Keuka Lake over a distance of 150 feet. Unfortunately, the originator, Samuel Pierpoint Langley, was not present to see his aircraft in flight. He had died in February, 1906.

The fact that Curtiss had redesigned the Langley flying boat and made false claims against the Wright brothers once again only served to increase the antagonism between two of America's greatest aviation pioneers. However, it did not stop Curtiss from developing one of his most successful aircraft, and one that would be a benchmark for flying boat design for the next two decades. In 1913, the Daily Mail newspaper in Great Britain had offered a £10,000 ($40,000) prize for the first non-stop airplane flight across the North Atlantic and Curtiss immediately took up the challenge. With his designer Rodman Wanamaker, Curtiss built his contender, the *America*, a large flying boat powered by two 160hp Curtiss Model V engines which was christened at Hammondsport in June 1914. The pilot chosen for the venture was a former British naval lieutenant and London agent for Deperdussin, John C Porte, who had been invalided out of the service with tuberculosis. After a successful first flight from Keuka

LEFT The Curtiss *America*, launched in June 1914, was designed for a transatlantic attempt by British pilot John Porte but was purchased by the British Admiralty after the outbreak of World War One.

RIGHT A Walsh flying boat of the New Zealand Flying School at Kohimarama, near Auckland which trained 110 pilots in New Zealand for the Royal Flying School during World War One.

Lake, Orville Wright threatened to take out an injunction to stop any Atlantic attempt unless Curtiss paid outstanding royalties for the misuse of the Wright company's patents. However, it was Germany's declaration of war in August 1914 that canceled any transatlantic attempts.

Before the end of the year, John Porte was able to persuade the British Admiralty to buy *America* and a second flying boat built as back-up for the planned Atlantic flight for use as anti-submarine patrol aircraft. Known in Royal Navy service as the Curtiss H.4 Little America, more than 60 of the American 'boats were delivered with twin 100hp Anzani engines in 1915. By this time, John Porte had re-joined the Royal Navy and was commander of the Royal Naval Air Station at Felixstowe in England, where the H.4s were accepted for service. Although extremely strong and reliable, the American 'boats were considered underpowered and not able to cope well with the high sea states of the North Sea. John Porte and his Seaplane Experimental Establishment were given the task of improving the H.4's hydrodynamic characteristics and this resulted in the F.1, the first in a line of successful of British Felixstowe flying boats.

FLYING BOATS AT WAR

At the outbreak of war, the recently formed Royal Naval Air Service (RNAS) possessed more aircraft than the Royal Flying Corps, which had been established in 1912. Several types of seaplane were pressed into service including the Short 184, more than 800 of which would be delivered by the end of the war, the Sopwith Tabloid, a production version of the 1914 Schneider winner which became the world's first single-seat military scout aircraft, and its more powerful development, the Sopwith Baby, one of the first aircraft to be fitted with flaps. A small two-seat flying boat of French design was built in Britain and used by the RNAS for training and observation. More than 150 of these Franco-British Aviation (FBA) 'boats were built. Although the United States had not yet entered the war, the US Navy was expanding its air service, mainly with Curtiss flying boats. A two-seat AB-2 'boat, the precursor of the HS-1/2 series of which more than 1,200 were eventually built for the US Navy, became the first aircraft to be catapulted when it was launched from the American battleship USS *North Carolina* anchored in Pensacola Bay, Florida on November 15, 1915. The US Navy also ordered a larger

version of the H.4 powered by two 350hp Liberty engines. The Curtiss H.12 carried a crew of four, was armed with three .300in Browning machine guns, and could carry up to 500lb of bombs or depth charges. In mid-1916 fifty H.12s fitted with 250hp Rolls-Royce Eagle engines and armed with .303in Lewis machine guns were ordered by the RNAS, where it became known as the Large America and was used as an anti-submarine patrol aircraft.

The use of flying boats as effective submarine-hunters was graphically illustrated on September 15, 1916 when the French submarine *Foucault* operating in the Adriatic was bombed and sunk by an Austro-Hungarian Navy Lohner flying boat which thus became the first aircraft to sink a submarine. The Austro-Hungarian Navy also produced one of the few flying boat "aces"

of the war, Lt Cdr Gottfried von Banfield, the commanding officer of the Trieste Naval Air Station, who claimed to have shot down some 20 French and Italian aircraft. Banfield flew more than 400 operational sorties over four years in a variety of flying boats including the Lohner and Hansa-Brandenburg W.18, although most of his victories were gained flying a specially modified Hansa-Brandenburg CC known as the *Blue Bird*. On April 6, 1917 the United States' declaration of war on Germany coincided with a dramatic increase in air activity over the North Sea with the introduction of the Large America, and its British-built development, the Felixstowe F.2a, into RNAS operations, and the appearance of the Imperial German Navy's formidable Hansa-Brandenburg floatplane fighter.

Two of the German fighters based at Zeebrugge in occupied Belgium successfully attacked and shot down in flames the British non-rigid airship C.17, operated by the Royal Navy, on April 21. Three weeks later, a Curtiss Large America from RNAS Great Yarmouth in Norfolk, England, flown by Flt Lt C J Galpin and Flt Sub-Lt R P Leckie, shot down the German naval Zeppelin L.22 off Texel in the Frisian Islands killing all 21 of the airship's crew.

A Large America from the same RNAS unit had the distinction of being the first aircraft to sink a German submarine when the flying boat piloted by Flt Sub-Lt C R Morrish bombed U-36 in the North Sea on May 20, 1917. Less than a month later, another spectacular victory was recorded by an H.12 from RNAS Great Yarmouth when Flt Sub-Lts Dicky and Hobbs shot down Zeppelin L.43 in flames when it was caught on a low-level scouting mission over the German-controlled sector of the North Sea off Ameland on June 14. All the airship's crew of 24 were killed.

A NARROW ESCAPE

The same Curtiss H.12 took off from Great Yarmouth on September 5 for an anti-Zeppelin patrol over Terschelling Island escorted by a two-seat DH.4 fighter. In command on that day was Sqn Cdr Nicholl who was flying with one of the unit's most experienced pilots, a Canadian flight sub-lieutenant, "Bob" Leckie, who had shot down Zeppelin L.22. Thirty miles from the Frisian Islands, two Zeppelins, L.44 and L.46, were spotted and attacked by the DH.4 flying at 12,000 feet. Return fire from the airships, which immediately turned southeast and climbed for safety, hit both the attacking aircraft. The DH.4's engine was damaged and its pilot had to break off the engagement and head back toward the English coast which was more than 75 miles away. The flying boat, meanwhile, continued its attack on L.44 but was at its maximum ceiling and it too gave up the chase after scoring several hits on the giant airship. The DH.4 had signalled to the H.12 by Aldis lamp that its engine had stopped and it was in a descending glide toward the waters of the North Sea.

On seeing the stricken landplane hit the water and the crew climb out of the sinking fighter, Leckie decided to land alongside

despite the flying boat's riddled hull. After a successful landing on the choppy sea, the downed crew were pulled aboard and Leckie attemped to take off. However, the flying boat had taken on a considerable amount of water during the landing and with one engine damaged during the air battle, it did not have enough

OPPOSITE A flight of multi-colored camouflaged RNAS Felixstowe F.2a flying boats, developed from the Curtiss H.12 by John Porte, attacking a German U-boat in the North Sea in 1917.

ABOVE An RNAS Curtiss H.12 Large America anti-submarine flying boat developed from the pre-war transatlantic contender America, being moored by its crew. Note the bombs carried under the wings.

power to get into the air. The only alternative was to taxi the 70-plus miles to England! As darkness fell, fuel was running low and the crews were only just bailing out fast enough to prevent the H.12 from foundering.

As they carried no radio, the only form of ship-to-shore communication was by carrier pigeon, four of which were carried aboard. Two birds were released on the first day and the remaining two on the second day. By now the boat was powerless and drifting northward. Although a massive air and sea search was underway, it was about to be called off when one of the carrier pigeons was found washed ashore dead near Lowestoft. The gunboat HMS *Halcyon* was the first ship to spot the half-submerged flying boat and picked up the six hungry and seasick crewmen at 2pm on September 8, more than three days after they began their patrol. The flying boat was also recovered and was

back in service a few weeks later about the same time as Zeppelin L.44 was shot down by French ack-ack guns over Arras after bombing England.

The fierce air battles over the North Sea continued unabated during the last year of hostilities. On December 11, 1917 three Brandenburg W.12s from Zeebrugge shot down the British coastal airship C.27 in flames over the North Sea, and on April 1, 1918 the RNAS amalgamated with the Royal Flying Corps to form the Royal Air Force (RAF), and the Boat Unit at Great Yarmouth became 228 Squadron. Shortly after, one of its Felixstowe F.2as was shot down by Zeebrugge Brandenburgs during an unescorted anti-U-boat patrol.

Five Felixstowe flying boats took on a dozen Brandenburgs off the German coast on June 4. In the battle, one F.2a was shot down and another was forced to land on the sea and taxi to

RIGHT The Felixstowe F.5 was the last of the line designed by Lt Cdr John Porte. It entered the RAF with 230 Squadron at Felixstowe in 1918, and influenced military flying boat design for almost two decades.

OPPOSITE Some of the most formidable floatplane fighters of the war, such as this Imperial German Navy W.29 which operated over the North Sea in 1918, were produced by the Hansa-Brandenburg company.

Holland, while the British 'boats, one of which was flown by "Bob" Leckie, claimed no less than six Brandenburgs. From mid-1918, the tide of the war began to change after four years of stagnation. German Zeppelins carried out their last raid on Britain on August 7, during which L.70, the Imperial German Navy's latest airship, was shot down in the sea off Norfolk by flying boat "ace" Capt "Bob" Leckie flying a DH.4 landplane. Over the next two months the Allies made steady gains and on October 28 elements of the Imperial German Navy mutinied and the service's naval air units were effectively grounded.

When World War One ended on November 11, 1918, the RAF had 125 Curtiss H.16 flying boats, a more powerful development of the H.12, on order but most were canceled. A similar number of Felixstowe F.2/3s were in production, but many of these were completed after the war as F.5s, the last of the line designed by John Porte featuring an improved wing structure.

Almost single-handedly, Glen Curtiss's flying boats and their British derivatives had proved to be highly capable warplanes and would influence the growth and development of maritime air operations over the next 25 years.

Aircraft design and technology had accelerated during the four years of World War One. However, the wood and fabric biplane remained predominant, with the greatest advances being made in developing powerful lightweight aero-engines.

LEFT The sleek Macchi M.52 failed to win the 1927 Schneider Trophy but Major Mario de Bernardi captured the absolute world air speed record in 1928 and finished runner-up in the 1929 contest.

ABOVE A Saro London I of 201 Squadron, motoring in to be beached at Calshot in 1936. Note that all six of the boat's crew are visible, as are the groundcrew who will fit the cumbersome beaching gear onto the aircraft.

SUPERMARINE SOUTHAMPTON MK I

Wooden-hulled RAF general reconnaissance flying boat with a crew of five belonging to 480 (Coastal Reconnaissance) Flight at Calshot in 1926.

STATISTICS

Wingspan	75ft
Length	51ft 1in
Height	22ft 4in
Weight	Empty 9,000lb Loaded 15,200lb
Engines	Two 502hp Napier Lion VA piston engines
Max speed	108mph
Cruise speed	98mph
Range	930 miles
Armament	3x.303in Lewis machine guns; 1,000lb bombload

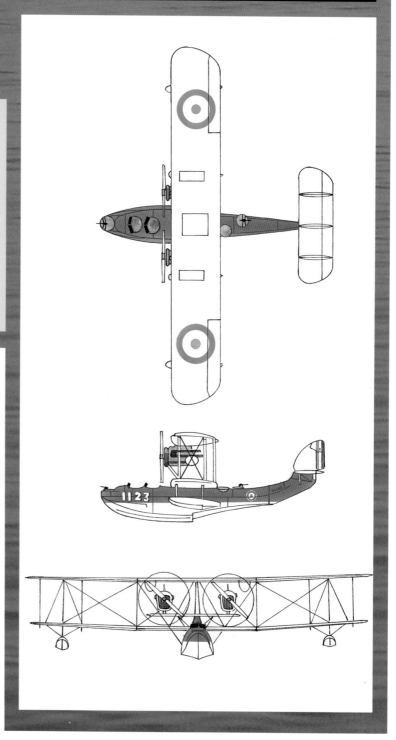

As pointers to future development of structural and aerodynamic trends in aircraft design, flying boats, and particularly those designed by Glen Curtiss and Ernst Heinkel, laid the foundations for the next decade. The Curtiss H.12 had been developed and refined by the British naval officer Lt John Porte and the Royal Navy's Seaplane Experimental Establishment at Felixstowe, from which the British-built Curtiss 'boats took their name.

It may be forgotten that a Curtiss flying boat, the US Navy's NC, was the first aircraft to fly the Atlantic ocean (completing Glen Curtiss's unfinished pre-war attempt), but ironically the future development of the flying boat in the dual roles of warplane and commercial airliner would be left to other companies on both sides of the Atlantic.

OPPOSITE PAGE The first Schneider winner to exceed the 200mph barrier was the Curtiss R3C-2, which won the 1925 contest averaging 232.57mph, piloted by the **US Army's Lt James "Jimmy" Doolittle.**

THE SCHNEIDER TROPHY

Heinkel's monoplane Hansa-Brandenburgs were the most successful seaplane fighters of the war. They were maneuverable, fast, and inspired a whole generation of Schneider Trophy contestants from the USA, Britain, and Italy. Immediately after the war, the entrants had been small flying boats, but it was again the Curtiss company that produced some sleek biplane racers on floats which gave the US Navy team victory in 1923 and 1925. In 1926, the Italians won with their streamlined Macchi M.39 low-wing monoplane floatplane.

The British team had adopted the same layout as the Italians in 1926 when R J Mitchell, Supermarine's chief designer, who was responsible for the 1922 contest-winning Supermarine Sea Lion II, produced the streamlined S.4. Although it met with an accident before the contest, which was won by the Italian Macchi team, the S.4 set a British seaplane speed record of 266.6mph. A year later the RAF competed for the first time with its High Speed Flight using the S.5, a development of the S.4 powered by

the well-tried and reliable 800hp Napier Lion engine. The slim clean lines of the S.5 were enhanced by the exceptionally thin wings and float struts, which had to be braced with wires for added strength, all of which cut drag to the minimum.

Held in September 1927 in front of a partisan crowd of over 200,000 in Venice, the beautiful but fragile Macchi M.52s had a variety of problems and the two British S.5s totally outclassed the opposition by finishing in first and second places. Flt Lt "Webby" Webster won the contest at an average speed of 281.65mph. The following year, the Italians were able to salvage some pride by breaking the world air speed record when the M.52 became the first aircraft to break the 300-mile-an-hour barrier, recording a speed of 318.57mph.

For his next Schneider design, Mitchell chose a Rolls-Royce engine in preference to the Napier powerplants used in the S.4 and S.5. The S.6 would be an all-metal monoplane powered by a new lightweight 1,900hp Rolls-Royce "R" (Racing) V12 engine which had to be designed and tested in six months if the aircraft was to take part in the 1929 contest. It was ready on time and the S.6 duly won the contest held at Spithead in England, almost in sight of the Supermarine works, and a few days later the same aircraft flown by Sqn Ldr A H Orlebar raised the world air speed record to 336.3mph.

The twelfth Schneider contest, again to be held in Britain at Spithead, featured the improved S.6B fitted with larger floats and a Rolls-Royce "R" engine boosted to 2,300hp. However, the Air Ministry, under pressure from the then Labour government, decided that, due to the depression, it could not fund the RAF's High Speed Flight or the British entry.

At this point Lady Houston entered the scene. The wealthy 74-year-old widow of Sir Richard Houston sent a telegram to the Prime Minister Ramsay MacDonald saying "the supremacy of English airmen can only be upheld by their entry in the Schneider Trophy, and as I consider this of supreme importance, I will guarantee the whole amount of £100,000 [the present-day equivalent of $10 million!] that you consider necessary."

In the event the French and Italian teams cried off at the last minute, so on September 12, 1931 the Schneider Trophy was won outright by Great Britain for all time by virtue of a third successive victory when Flt Lt J N Boothman completed the course at a speed of 349.08mph. To reinforce its victory, the same S.6B gained the world air speed record when Flt Lt G H Stainforth recorded a speed of 407.5mph, the seaplane becoming the first aircraft in the world to break the 400mph barrier.

The Italians continued to develop their unsuccessful 1931 Schneider challenger, the Macchi M.72, and their efforts were rewarded with a new absolute world speed record of 440.68mph on October 24, 1934. Floatplane technology had now reached its zenith and all future world speed records would be broken by landplanes. However, R J Mitchell used the lessons learned from his trophy-winning seaplanes to lay the foundations of his most memorable design—the Supermarine Spitfire—while a series of Macchi fighters used by the Italians during the early years of World War Two were clearly influenced by the M.52 and M.67 Schneider contestants.

Although the American Schneider challenge faded after its failure to win the 1926 contest held at Hampton Roads in the USA, the Curtiss R3C floatplanes were the progenitor of the famous Hawk series of fighters which were the mainstay of the US Army and Marine Corps during the 1930s.

LEFT The RAF's High Speed Flight won the Schneider Trophy outright in 1931 with the streamlined Supermarine S.6B designed by R J Mitchell, who was the designer of the Battle of Britain Spitfire.

OPPOSITE FAR RIGHT The four-engine US Navy Curtiss NC-4 was the first aircraft to fly across the Atlantic in May 1919 when it was the only one of three that completed the flight from Canada to Portugal via the Azores.

OPPOSITE RIGHT The winner of an Air Ministry competition for a fleet support amphibian in 1920, the wooden-hull Vickers Viking IV powered by a single Napier Lion engine was adopted by the Argentine Navy.

CROSSING THE OCEANS

However, it was the Curtiss flying boat designs of World War One which influenced RAF flying boats for almost two decades between the wars. It was a US Navy Curtiss (NC) flying boat that was the first aircraft to cross the Atlantic. Three of the 126-foot wingspan biplanes powered by four 400hp Liberty engines, took off from Trepassey, Newfoundland on May 16, 1919 but two of them had to make forced landings in the Atlantic before they

reached their scheduled refuelling stop in the Azores. Both crews were rescued by US Navy warships while Lt Cdr Albert Read successfully completed the 1,400-mile leg to Horta Harbor in the Azores in 15 hours and 13 minutes. Two days later, NC-4 left for Ponta Delgada, Lisbon and reached Plymouth, England on May 31 at the end of a 3,925-mile flight completed in 57 hours and 16 minutes. The Curtiss was escorted into Plymouth harbor by three RAF Felixstowe F.2As, themselves developments of the Curtiss H.12 flying boat. Post-war development of John Porte's twin-engined F-boats was continued by Short Brothers after Porte's untimely death in October 1919. In 1921, the RAF had more than 100 Felixstowe boats on strength including 25 of the latest F.5s, which equipped nine squadrons in the UK and Malta.

Unfortunately, Glen Curtiss was about to lose control of his pioneering company when it merged with the Wright company,

partly owned by his arch rival, Orville Wright. Curtiss retired from the aviation business in 1920 and tragically died following an emergency operation for appendicitis 10 years later.

One of the first post-war British flying boat designs was the Vickers Viking, a neat two-seat single-engine biplane design which gained some unwelcome publicity when Sir John Alcock, recently knighted along with his co-pilot Arthur Whitten Brown for making the first non-stop transatlantic flight in June 1919, was killed when he crashed in fog while delivering a new Viking to France. In 1920, the Air Ministry's Advisory Committee for Aeronautics organized a competition for a new British amphibian design. A Viking III fitted with a folding undercarriage won the first prize of £10,000 ($40,000) and, although the type was not adopted by the RAF, Viking IVs were sold to the navies of France, the Netherlands, Russia, and the Argentine.

More successful was the single-engine Seagull amphibian designed by R J Mitchell, who was responsible for the Supermarine Sea Lion that crashed in the 1919 Schneider contest but went on to win it in 1922. The two-seat deck-landing amphibian which first flew in 1922 marked the emergence of Supermarine as a military constructor. The Seagull would be continually developed over the following decade, with the line remaining in RAF service until 1946!

Mitchell's next military design was the twin-engine Southampton, the first of which replaced 230 Squadron's Felixstowe F.5s in 1925. A total of 78 Southamptons were built for the RAF, the first six of which had wooden hulls while the remaining Mark IIs had metal hulls. The type was to boost the

TOP R J Mitchell's first military flying boat design was the Southampton II, 78 of which served with six squadrons including 205 Squadron which operated S1043 at Seletar in 1930.

ABOVE One of four Supermarine Southampton IIs belonging to the RAF's Far East Flight that undertook a 27,000-mile cruise to Hong Kong from Felixstowe via the Mediterranean, India, and Singapore in 1927 to 1928.

cash-strapped RAF's reputation as a professional pioneering service when its Southamptons quickly captured the headlines with a series of long-distance cruises. Between October 1927 and December 1928 four of the twin 502hp Napier Lion-powered flying boats of the Far East Flight flew from Felixstowe, England to Singapore and Hong Kong via the Mediterranean and India, a total of 27,000 miles. The following year 205 Squadron flew a 19,500-mile return flight to Singapore and the Andaman Islands.

A development of the Southampton fitted with an enclosed cockpit and powered by two 525hp Rolls-Royce Kestrel engines, the Scapa flew in 1933 but only 31 were delivered to the RAF. However, the "Flying Boat Union" was now a powerful faction within the RAF and was able to place contracts for new types while the fighter and bomber force had to rely on updated versions of World War One designs.

THE NEXT GENERATION

The service had a requirement for a more powerful, longer-range flying boat and an Air Ministry specification issued in 1924 was successfully met by the Blackburn Iris, which first flew in September 1926. Powered by three 675hp Rolls-Royce Condor engines, the all-metal Iris III had a wingspan of 97 feet and carried a crew of five in some comfort. Armed with three .303 machine guns and able to carry a 2,200lb bombload, the Iris III was christened "Britain's Aerial Battleship."

Unfortunately, the big flying boat was not an unqualified success in service. It was the Blackburn company's first large flying boat design and, at £60,000 ($240,000) each, production was limited to only four aircraft, enough to equip just one squadron, 209 Squadron based at Mount Batten, Plymouth. Two of the flying boats crashed in Plymouth Sound, both making world news. The first, in 1931, resulted in the RAF's biggest loss of life to date when Iris N238 carrying a double crew of 12 hit a submerged object and sank with the loss of nine lives. One of the first on the scene was Aircraftsman Shaw who dived into the water and helped rescue one of the survivors by supporting him until he could be lifted from the water and rushed to hospital.

Shaw, who was better known at the time as "Lawrence of Arabia," had joined the RAF to get out of the limelight but was now back in the headlines.

The second accident occurred in January 1933 when Iris S1263, which had been upgraded to the Mark V specification with a covered cockpit and more powerful Rolls-Royce Buzzard engines and had been renamed a Perth, crashed on take-off following an engine failure. One crew member was killed and the flying boat was written off. The remaining two re-engined Iris Vs and four newly-built Perths were withdrawn from service in 1935.

The first Short Brothers flying boat to enter RAF service was a military version of one of Imperial Airways' first flying boat airliners, the Calcutta. Six three-engine Short Rangoons were used by 203 Squadron stationed at Basra, Iraq from 1931, flying long sorties throughout the Persian Gulf watching for gun-runners and smugglers. In 1934 three of the Rangoons left for a 19,000-mile cruise to Australia and back. None had been lost when the type was replaced by its successor, the Short Singapore in 1936.

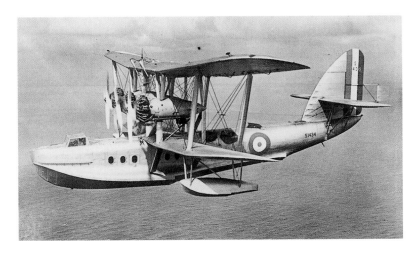

ABOVE The Short Rangoon was unusual in that it was developed from an Imperial Airways commercial airliner, the Calcutta. Powered by three 540hp Bristol Jupiter XI engines, it served with 203 Squadron in Iraq.

ABOVE RIGHT While in service with 209 Squadron at Mount Batten, Plymouth, the Blackburn Iris III was the RAF's largest aircraft. S1263 crashed in Plymouth Sound in 1933, killing one of its crew of five.

Powered by four 700hp Rolls-Royce Kestrel engines in tandem pairs, the Singapore III had a maximum speed of 136 mph and a range of 1,235 miles. A total of 37 production aircraft equipped six RAF squadrons and operated in the Mediterranean during the Italian invasion of Abyssinia in 1935, and two years later Singapores of 209 and 210 Squadrons flew patrols from Malta and Algeria over British shipping during the Spanish Civil War.

Other RAF flying boats of the period included further developments of Mitchell's Southampton, the last of the Supermarine line being the Stranraer. This first flew in 1935 and featured a new swept wing and two 980hp Bristol Pegasus X engines, giving it almost twice the power of the Southampton I. One of the last biplane designs to enter RAF service was the Saro London, a general reconnaissance boat powered by two 1,055hp Bristol Pegasus X engines with a maximum speed of 155mph. The first of 13 Londons entered service in April 1936, replacing the Scapa. Between November 1937 and May 1938, five Londons of 204 Squadron based at Plymouth and fitted with long-range fuel tanks made a 30,000-mile flight to New South Wales and back. The type was also involved in patrolling the Mediterranean during the Spanish Civil War.

An important type that never hit the headlines was the Saro Cloud, a small twin-engine monoplane amphibian which was

adopted by the RAF in 1930 as a flying boat trainer. Sixteen Clouds powered by two 340hp Armstrong Siddeley Double Mongoose engines had an enclosed cockpit for an instructor and student pilot while its spacious cabin was fitted out as a flying classroom for training up to eight navigators. The type equipped the Seaplane Training Squadron at Calshot, the School of Air Pilotage at Andover, and 48 Squadron at Manston. Gun mountings could be fitted in the bow and aft compartments and four 50lb practice bombs could be carried under the wings. This adaptable and reliable flying boat gave excellent service throughout its 10-year RAF career.

PASSENGERS AND POST

Although the military development of the flying boat broke new grounds during the inter-war years, many forget that early European air transport was also undertaken by the flying boat. Marine aircraft were in widescale service during the 1920s in the Adriatic, the Baltic, the Mediterranean, and the Swiss and Italian lakes. One of the most successful aircraft of the period was designed by one of the flying boat's greatest proponents, Claudius Dornier. At the end of World War One, the Inter-Allied Control Commission (IACC) was set up with the express aim of preventing the defeated powers from creating new arms industries; this precluded the production of any aircraft. To circumvent the IACC, German designers established aviation companies overseas. These included Ernst Heinkel, designer of the Hansa-Brandenburg fighter seaplanes, who moved to Sweden, Professor Hugo Junkers, who moved to Russia, and Heinrich Rohrbach, who moved to Denmark.

In the meantime, Claudius Dornier had produced the first Wal flying boat at Marina di Pisa in Italy, an aircraft that would revolutionize air travel in Europe. The metal-hulled parasol monoplane flying boat powered by two 300hp Hispano-Suiza engines in tandem first flew on November 6, 1922 with the first

TOP One of the few monoplane flying boats in RAF service between the wars was the neat Saro Cloud amphibian which was used to train pilots and navigators of the RAF's big boats.

RIGHT The penultimate updated version of the Southampton was the Supermarine Scapa. One of only 14 built in 1933, K1491 belonged to 202 Squadron based in Malta.

CENTER RIGHT The first Dornier Wal (whale), which flew from Marina de Pisa in Italy for the first time in November 1922, was one of 16 delivered to the Spanish Air Force.

order for the type being placed by the Spanish Air Force, which eventually operated 16 Wals. Its two spacious cabins could accommodate up to 14 passengers, and operators were offered the choice of a dozen different engines ranging from the 360hp Rolls-Royce Eagle IX to the 600hp Siemens Sh.20.

Its outstanding seaworthiness, reliability, and simplicity of maintenance made the Wal a favourite with both air forces and commercial airlines. It was also involved in a series of pioneering long-distance flights which led to its being produced under license in Spain, the Netherlands, and Japan.

In 1925, two Wals were used by the Amundsen–Ellsworth Polar Expedition in an attempt to fly to the North Pole. When the flight had to be abandoned due to bad weather, the whole expedition was flown off the ice by one of the Wals and taken to Norway. In January 1926, a Spanish Air Force Wal flew 6,259 miles from Spain to Buenos Aires in 59 hours 35 minutes, the first South Atlantic flight in an east–west direction. The German airline Lufthansa used three upgraded J Wals to pioneer its South Atlantic mail services in 1930 using aviation support ships based off the coasts of West Africa and South America which could refuel the flying boats and catapult them on to their destination. Lufthansa's first scheduled transatlantic flight from Berlin,

ABOVE The all-metal monoplane Wal had two comfortable cabins for up to 14 passengers. This Wal with Rolls-Royce Eagle engines was used by the Italian airline SANA on the Genoa–Rome–Naples–Palermo route.

Germany to Buenos Aires, Argentina took off on February 3, 1934 carrying 105lb of mail. The 2,200-mile flight across the Atlantic took 13 hours, and by July 1935 Lufthansa J Wals had made their hundredth South Atlantic crossing, having carried four million items of mail on the route.

Another Lufthansa J Wal made a round-the-world flight via Iceland, Greenland, Canada, USA, Japan, China, India, Persia, and the Mediterranean between July and November 1932. More than a dozen other airlines used the Wal on scheduled passenger services in Europe, South America, Japan, and Indonesia. Military Wals, known as the Do 15, were operated by the clandestine Luftwaffe and the Royal Netherlands Navy, bringing the total number built between 1922 and 1934 to 264. While the Wal was establishing the reputation of being one of the most advanced and successful water-borne aircraft of the 1920s and early 1930s, Claudius Dornier was designing a giant version of the Wal capable

of carrying 66 passengers non-stop across the Atlantic. Based on his projected R-type flying boat designed for the Imperial German Navy during World War One, the Do X had a wingspan of 157 feet 6 inches, a length of 131 feet 5 inches, weighed 48 tons, and was powered by no less than twelve 525hp Siemens Jupiter engines in tandem pairs. Again, to avoid the tight restrictions imposed on the production of aircraft in Germany by the Treaty of Versailles, construction of the huge flying boat began at Altenrhein on the Swiss shore of Lake Constance in December 1927. It took some 750 workers a year and a half to complete the prototype Do X, the largest heavier-than-air flying machine the world had ever seen, which made its first flight on July 29, 1929. Three months later it made the headlines again by making a one-hour flight over Lake Constance with 169 people aboard—10 crew, 150 passengers, and nine stowaways!

After making more than 300 test flights, its original engines were replaced by 600hp Curtiss Conqueror GV-1870 V-12 engines in August 1930 in an effort to improve its performance. On November 5, 1930 the Do X left for a protracted demonstration flight over four continents. Its route followed the Rhine down to Amsterdam, from there to Calshot (England), Bordeaux (France), La Coruña (Spain), and Lisbon (Portugal). Here fire damaged the port wing and an aborted take-off caused further damage to the hull. After lengthy repairs, the Dornier finally flew to Portuguese Guinea in West Africa via the Canary Islands on May 1, 1939. On June 20, after a 13-hour flight across the South Atlantic via Natal, the Dornier reached Rio de Janeiro before leaving for Antigua, Miami, and New York where it arrived on August 27. After spending the winter at New York airport, the Do X took off in May 1932 for the flight back to Germany via Newfoundland, the

OPPOSITE LEFT This famous Wal, seen against the New York waterfront in 1930, had been used to rescue the Amundsen–Ellsworth Polar Expedition from the ice in 1925 after an aborted flight to the North Pole.

BELOW This Italian-built Wal powered by two BMW VI engines in tandem and fitted with round windows was delivered to the German airline Lufthansa in 1925.

RIGHT Lufthansa's 8-ton J Wal *Monsun* being lifted onto the catapult of one of the airline's aviation support ships prior to a South Atlantic mail flight from Bathurst to Natal in 1933.

BELOW Lufthansa's only Dornier Do X transatlantic flying boat, which was the largest aircraft in the world when it first flew from Lake Constance in July 1929.

ABOVE One of two Rolls-Royce Eagle-engined Dornier Wals that was used by the ill-fated Amundsen-Ellsworth Polar Expedition in 1924/5.

LEFT The Do X, seen on its arrival at Calshot from Amsterdam on the second leg of its transatlantic flight in November 1930. Note the twelve 600hp Curtiss Conqueror engines fitted back-to-back.

OPPOSITE RIGHT The captain's bridge on the Dornier Do X flying boat, showing the huge control and trimming wheels, the minimum of instruments, and the thermos flask strapped in front of the pilot's left-hand seat.

OPPOSITE FAR RIGHT The plush upholstered chairs, walnut panelling, Persian rugs, and oriental wallpaper that adorned the main passenger cabin aboard the Dornier Do X flying boat rivalled any luxury liner of the time.

Azores, and Calshot to land on the Buggelsee in Berlin on May 24 having covered 22,000 miles in 211 flying hours.

Although the flying colossus had proved to be, like its smaller relatives, exceptionally seaworthy it was seriously underpowered and, after being delivered to Lufthansa in May 1933, was found to be uneconomical and was withdrawn from service after less than a year. Two more Do Xs had been built for the Italian airline SANA, which operated some 20 Wals, for services over the Trieste– Venice–Genoa–Marseilles–Barcelona–Cartagena–Gibraltar route. Powered by twelve 550hp Fiat V-12 engines, the two SANA flying boats were delivered to Genoa in 1932 but by this time the worldwide economic crisis had begun to bite and the Italian Do Xs were never used by the airline but passed to the military during the following year.

OTHER DEVELOPMENTS

Dornier was not the only German designer trying to produce a viable transatlantic commercial flying boat in the 1920s. Adolf Rohrbach had set up business in Denmark in 1922, again to avoid the attention of the Inter-Allied Control Commission, and developed a range of twin-engine flying boats. The Rocco and Rodra, designed by a youthful Kurt Tank who was later to design

one of the Luftwaffe's most successful World War Two fighters— the Fw 190—were used in small numbers on Lufthansa's Baltic routes in the late 1920s. A larger three-engine development was designed for the transatlantic route carrying 20 passengers, but after extensive trials in 1928–29 the technically advanced Romar proved it did not have the legs to be an Atlantic contender and joined its smaller stablemates on the Baltic run. Despite the IACC, two Rodras were purchased by the British government for RAF evaluation in 1927, where it was known as the Beardmore Inverness, but later scrapped.

Italy and France both produced a number of commercially successful flying boats in the inter-war period. The Macchi company developed a series of small passenger-carrying 'boats from wartime military aircraft before concentrating on its Schneider Trophy racers, but it was the Savoia-Marchetti flying boats that took part in one of the most spectacular transatlantic flights of all time. To celebrate Benito Mussolini's tenth anniversary in power, no less than 25 SM.55X flying boats flew from Italy to America in 1933—in formation. Commanded by the Italian Minister of Air, General Italo Balbo, who had already led 10 SM.55 torpedo bombers across the South Atlantic in January 1931, the Italian formation took off from Orbetello seaplane base

near the Italian capital, Rome, on July 1, 1933 en route for Amsterdam, where one crashed on landing.

The remaining 24 twin-engine twin-hull flying boats flew on to the Century of Progress Exposition in Chicago via Ireland, Iceland, Labrador, and New Brunswick, Canada, and they all landed safely despite appalling weather en route. The aircrews were hand-picked air force pilots who had trained for more than a year on the S.55s and the whole flight was supported across the ocean by ships of the Italian Navy. After a 10-day stopover in the United States the formation returned to Italy via Lisbon where another 'boat was lost, before the 23 survivors touched down on the River Tiber to national acclaim on August 12. This success led to the development of a three-engine twin-hull commercial flying boat, the SM.66, which could carry 18 passengers and a crew of three; 24 of these were produced between 1932 and 1934.

France also experimented with transatlantic flying boats, the most successful of which were designed by the Latecoere company. The four-engine Late 300 made several South Atlantic

crossings for Air France via Dakar and Natal between 1933 and December 1938, when it was lost with its crew of three. The company then produced the Type 521, a six-engine giant almost as large as the Do X. Christened *Lieutenant de Vaisseau Paris*, the Late 521 first flew in January 1935 and made a successful maiden flight to the United States via the Caribbean a year later. However, it was damaged by a hurricane and sank in Pensacola Bay, Florida. It was later salvaged, dismantled, and shipped back to France where it was rebuilt and re-engined with six 650hp Hispano-Suiza 12N engines before resuming trials in late 1937. The Late 521, designed to carry 70 passengers and a crew of eight, broke the seaplane distance record by flying 3,591.5 miles in 34 hours 37 minutes in November 1937 and flew to New York via Lisbon and the Azores in August 1938. Unfortunately, Air France's plans to open a scheduled Paris to New York passenger service were stopped by the outbreak of World War Two in September 1939.

OPPOSITE The twin-hulled Savoia-Marchetti S.55X Italian Air Force torpedo bomber made famous by General Italo Balbo's mass-formation flights across the South Atlantic in 1931 followed by the North Atlantic in 1933.

RIGHT Air France LeO H242 *Ville d'Oran* arriving at Marseilles after a flight from Algiers in 1935.

OPPOSITE FAR LEFT Developed from the World War One Franco-British Aviation boats, the adaptable French Schreck 17 served both as a three-passenger civil aircraft and a military flying boat trainer throughout the 1920s and 1930s.

OPPOSITE BELOW LEFT The only German flying boat manufacturer to rival Dornier in the 1920s and 1930s was Rohrbach, which built a number of high-tech two- and three-engine monoplane boats, such as the *Rocco*, for Lufthansa.

RIGHT Developed from the S.55, the three-engine S.66 commercial flying boat carried up to 18 passengers in its twin-hulled cabins and was operated by two Italian airlines on Mediterranean services in the 1930s.

THE ENDS OF EMPIRE

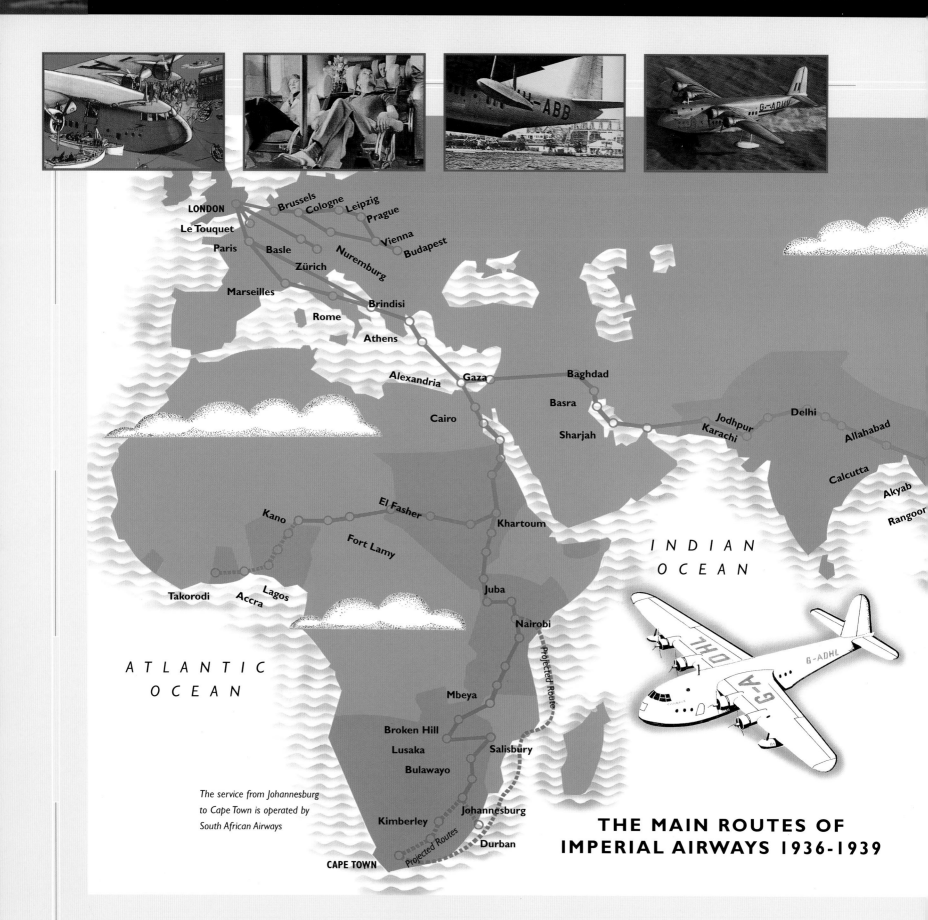

LONDON
Brussels · Cologne · Leipzig
Le Touquet
Prague
Paris
Basle
Vienna
Zürich
Nuremburg
Budapest
Marseilles
Brindisi
Rome
Athens
Alexandria · Gaza · Baghdad
Cairo · Basra
Sharjah
Jodhpur · Delhi
Karachi
Allahabad
Calcutta
Akyab
El Fasher
Khartoum
Rangoon
Kano
Fort Lamy
Juba
INDIAN
OCEAN
Takorodi · Accra · Lagos
Nairobi
ATLANTIC
OCEAN
Mbeya
Broken Hill
Salisbury
Lusaka
Bulawayo

The service from Johannesburg
to Cape Town is operated by
South African Airways

Kimberley
Johannesburg
Durban
CAPE TOWN
Projected Routes

THE MAIN ROUTES OF
IMPERIAL AIRWAYS 1936-1939

HONG KONG

ngkok Tourane

Saigon

enang

Singapore

Batavia

Rambang

Koepang Darwin

Normanton

Cloncurry

BRISBANE

Charleville

PACIFIC
OCEAN

With the flying boat now accepted as the most suitable option for long-haul commercial air travel, governments set about establishing state-supported airlines that would open up the world as never before. To these ends, Britain formed Imperial Airways in 1924 by merging four private short-haul airlines; the stated aim of the new airline was to be the key factor in linking up Britain's worldwide Empire.

LEFT The far flung reaches of the British Empire were brought together for the first time when Imperial Airways' "C" class flying boats began scheduled services from Southampton to South Africa and Australia in the 1930s.

ABOVE Imperial Airways' first commercial flying boat was the Supermarine Sea Eagle, two of which were taken on charge when the airline was formed in 1924.

SHORT S.17 KENT

Medium-range commerical flying boat with a crew of four built for Imperial Airways to operate the Empire Routes in 1932.

STATISTICS

Wingspan	113ft
Length	78ft 5in
Height	28ft
Weight	Empty 20,460lb Loaded 32,000lb
Engines	Four 555hp Bristol Jupiter XFBM radials
Max speed	110mph
Cruise speed	105mph
Range	450 miles
Passengers	Maximum 16

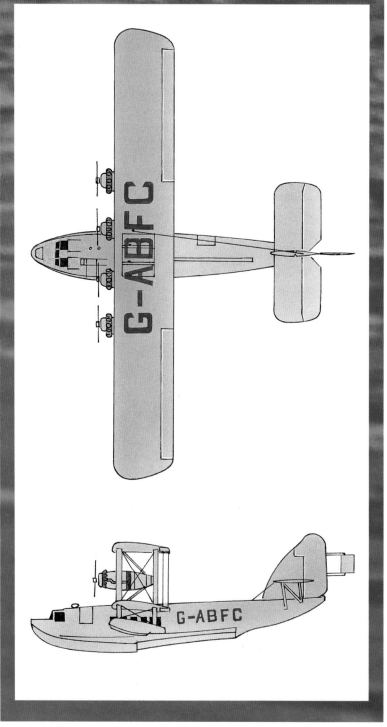

REGULAR SERVICES

Having benefited from the experience gained by the RAF's long-range flying boat survey flights, the new airline ordered a small fleet of three-engine long-range Short Calcutta flying boats developed from the RAF's Singapore I to operate sectors of Imperial's proposed air route to India. At the end of 1928, air pioneer Sir Alan Cobham set off on a 23,000 mile survey flight of the London–South Africa route on behalf of Imperial Airways in a former RAF Singapore flying boat.

The following year, Imperial Calcuttas began operating the trans-Mediterranean sector of the England to India route, and these were supplemented in 1931 by three Short Kent four-engine biplane flying boats that could carry 16 passengers in considerable comfort complete with a well-equipped galley for cooking hot meals in mid-flight.

However, it was the Post Office that opened up the world to long-distance air travel in the 1930s when the British Postmaster

General introduced the government's Empire Postal Scheme which announced that airmail letters could be sent between any of the countries within the British Empire for only one-and-a-half old pence (2.5 cents) an ounce.

This resulted in Imperial Airways placing an unprecedented £1.75 million ($7 million) contract with Short Brothers at Rochester, England, for 28 four-engine flying boats straight off the drawing board in 1935. The first of the giant Short S-23 flying boats, known by the airline as the Empire "C" Class, took to the air from the River Medway on July 4, 1936.

The all-metal monoplane "C" Class flying boats had an extremely advanced design. Its deep streamlined hull gave a spacious interior, while the four 910hp Bristol Pegasus engines which merged into the wing gave it a maximum range of 1,500 miles at a cruising speed of 160mph. The latest Gouge wingflaps gave the big 'boat a significantly shorter take-off and landing run on water than the smaller biplanes it replaced. Although capable of seating 24 day passengers and sleeping 19 with a crew of five, the Empire 'boats carried only 17 passengers on the longer routes in order to carry one-and-a-half tons of luggage and airmail.

At the same time, Imperial Airways sponsored the building of a novel composite aircraft, designed by Major Mayo, that would be capable of flying from London to New York non-stop. This was simply a slightly smaller version of the "C" Class flying boat, the S.21 *Maia*, that would carry aloft a smaller four-engine seaplane, the S.20 *Mercury*, on its back. *Maia* was designed to take off with the fully fueled *Mercury* locked in place above its main wing with its engines started. After becoming airborne and climbing to 5,000 feet, the pair would separate.

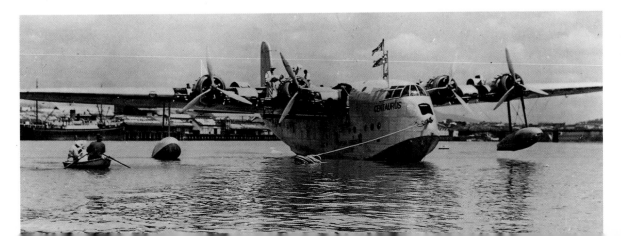

BELOW Short S.23 *Centaurus* was the third of Imperial Airways' "C" Class Empire Boats. It was launched at Rochester, England on October 29, 1936 and was the first one to fly to Australia in November 1937.

TOP Imperial Airways' first 12-passenger Short Calcutta *City of Alexandria*, seen on the Thames in August 1928 prior to the opening of the airline's England to India route.

ABOVE The luxurious four-engine Short Kent airliner named *Scipio* entered service on the Genoa to Alexandria sector of Imperial Airways' route to India in April 1931.

On July 21, 1938, the pair separated over Foynes, Ireland, and *Mercury*, flown by Capt "Don" Bennett and carrying 600lbs of mail, flew to Montreal, Canada, a distance of 2,930 miles in 20 hours 20 minutes. Following this successful flight, it was decided that the Short–Mayo composite should be used to attempt to break the world's seaplane distance record. *Mercury* was launched from *Maia* over Dundee in Scotland on October 6, 1939, again with Capt Bennett at the controls. Just over 42 hours later, Bennett and his co-pilot Capt Harvey touched down on the Orange River in South Africa having flown 5,997.5 miles non-stop—a seaplane record that has never been broken.

LUXURY IN THE AIR

Meanwhile, the "C" Class 'boats began to fly the London to Sydney route in June 1938 with nightstops at Athens, Basra, Karachi, Calcutta, Bangkok, Singapore, Surabaya, Darwin, and Townsville. In 1938 the trip took nine days, compared with 30 days by ocean liner, and cost £274 ($1,100) return!

For this price, the then equivalent of a small house, the privileged few passengers flew first class, which in those days meant exactly that. Accommodation aboard the flying boat included two spacious passenger cabins, a promenade cabin,

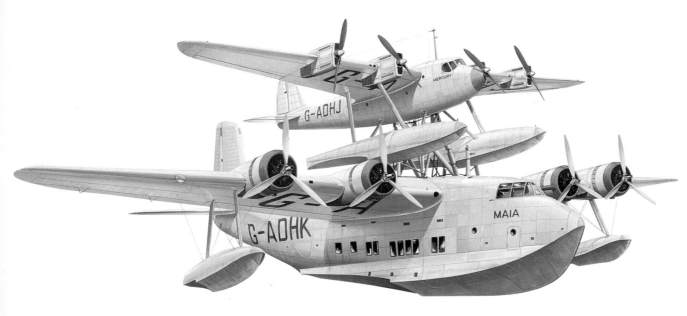

TOP LEFT *Cambria* was the second long-range S.23 Empire Boat entering service with Imperial Airways in January 1937. It survived the war only to be scrapped in 1946.

CENTER LEFT An evocative shot of *Cambria* taking off in its wartime markings after being converted to austerity standard seating for 29 passengers and being put on the "Horseshoe Route" in 1940.

LEFT The Short–Mayo composite with the seaplane *Mercury* mounted on *Maia* in the Medway prior to its record-breaking flights to Canada and South Africa in 1938.

separate ladies' and gentlemen's lavatories, a small but select wine cellar, and a large galley. Apart from a flight deck crew of five—pilot, co-pilot, navigator, flight engineer, and wireless operator—two stewards saw to the passengers' every need. The captain often joined passengers for lunch cooked by the stewards in the galley. Menus of the time included pâté de foie gras, ox tongue, York ham, roast fillet of lamb, poached salmon écosse, salads, peach melba, figs, and even crêpes Suzette.

Passengers began their journey by booking their luggage in at the Imperial Airways booking hall at Victoria Station before travelling by train to Southampton the evening before the flight was due to leave. After an overnight stay at a first-class hotel and a leisurely breakfast, the adventure would begin. Despite the luxurious menus and overnight stops at five-star hotels, passengers had to be resilient as well as wealthy. The Empire Boats were slow, noisy, and unpressurized which meant they were unable to climb above sandstorms, bumpy air pockets created by the heat of the tropics, and monsoon rains. On the Australian route, they had to endure 29 landings and take-offs, many of which were under the sweltering midday sun and often in bad weather. Imperial Airways also flew a twice-weekly London to Cape Town route with its Empire Boats.

Although a number of the "C" Class flying boats came to grief in the two years they flew the Empire routes, only six passengers lost their lives. Others had close scrapes in remote parts of the world including *Ceres* which had to make an emergency landing on a small lake between Karachi and Calcutta in June 1938 after running short of fuel due to strong headwinds. Although there were no injuries, the passengers and their luggage had to be offloaded to continue to the next port of call on bullock carts and trains before the lightened flying boat was able to take off two

days later. *Corsair* hit rocks attempting to take off from a river in the Congo en route from Lake Victoria to Juba in March 1939. Although again there were no casualties, the long-suffering passengers had to continue their journey by train once again, but it would take airline engineers nine months to repair the flying boat on site before it could be flown back to Hythe in England!

Other "C" Class flying boats were sold to the Australian airline QANTAS, while two larger S.30s and three long-range "G" Class aircraft were built in 1939. The latter, with more powerful engines and a range of 3,200 miles carrying 38 passengers, were designed for the North Atlantic route. Imperial Airways' S.23 *Caledonia* had made the airline's first North Atlantic survey flight from Hythe to

TOP RIGHT Passengers aboard an Empire Boat in 1938 playing cards at the start of their 5,029-mile flight to India which would take four days and involve 14 stops.

RIGHT Empire Boat *Caster* seen on its step during take-off from Hythe, England. Launched in December 1937, it flew the last "C" Class service from India in January 1947.

Botwood, Newfoundland on July 5–6, 1937, and with the benefit of aerial refueling developed by the aviation pioneer, Sir Alan Cobham, the first "C" Class boat, named *Cabot*, flew mail on a 13-hour flight from Poole to Botwood, Newfoundland, in September of 1939 en route for New York.

Capt "Don" Bennett flew Imperial Airways' first England to Canada service with *Cabot*, via Foynes and Botwood, on August 17, 1939 and, although the Empire Boats flew a twice-weekly five-hour service from New York to Bermuda between 1937 and 1939, it was a Pan American flying boat, the giant Boeing 314, that flew the first regular transatlantic passenger service between New York and London on June 28, 1939.

The outbreak of World War Two put paid to Imperial's North Atlantic passenger service but its Empire Boats were to continue flying with the RAF and British Overseas Airways Corporation (BOAC) for another six years.

WAR AGAIN

On April 1, 1940 BOAC was formed with the merger of Imperial Airways and the short-haul pre-war airline, British Airways. The new airline inherited 21 surviving "C" Class flying boats, three of the recently delivered Short S.26 "G" Class 'boats and two S.33s still in production at Rochester, England. Powered by four 1,380hp Bristol Hercules IV engines and having a four-man flight crew, the long-range S.26s had not entered revenue service with Imperial Airways and were almost immediately pressed into service with the RAF as North Atlantic patrol aircraft, as were two S.30s, *Cabot* and *Clio*. Both of these were sunk by the Luftwaffe during the battle of Norway in May 1940 while two of the S.26s were lost in wartime accidents.

In BOAC service the "C" Class 'boats operated a lifeline between Britain and the Empire based on some of the old Imperial routes, particularly those to South Africa, and India and Australia via East Africa. An important new route introduced in the first year of the war was to Freetown in West Africa, flown via neutral Lisbon. The Empire Boats moved from Hythe to their wartime base at Poole in Dorset in 1940 and most were converted to basic accommodation for 29 day passengers and maximum cargo.

With Italy entering the war and the fall of France in June 1940, refueling stops within the first 1,500 miles of the Empire

TOP LEFT Imperial Airways Empire Boat *Challenger* crashed in Mozambique harbor en route from South Africa on May 1, 1939, killing two of the crew.

TOP RIGHT The first S.23 delivered to **QANTAS** was *Coolangatta*, which arrived in Australia on March 18, 1938, from Southampton. She later served with the **RAAF** as a sub-hunter.

LEFT The liner *Capetown Castle* at Southampton in April 1938, prior to its maiden voyage to South Africa which would take two weeks, while the Empire Boat *Circe* would make the same trip in five days.

TOP LEFT The long-range S.30 Cabot seen venting fuel during air refuelling trials with Sir Alan Cobham's company in 1939, was sunk at Bodo in Norway serving with the RAF in May 1940.

TOP RIGHT Imperial Airways passengers being ferried to "C" Class Empire boat *Capella* at Hythe, in 1930. She was wrecked at Batavia in March 1939 with no casualties.

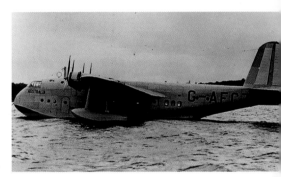

CENTER RIGHT Launched as *Australia* for the New Zealand airline TEAL in 1939, the S.30 was damaged on delivery at Basra and transferred to Imperial Airways as *Clare* to fly the transatlantic route in 1940.

RIGHT In September 1937, Empire Boat *Ceres* surveyed the Alexandria to Karachi route but was later wrecked by an explosion during maintenance in South Africa in December 1942.

routes including Biscarosse, Marseilles, Rome, Brindisi, and Ajaccio were lost. Initially they were replaced by Gibraltar and Malta, but as the Germans, aided by the Italians, tightened their grip around the Mediterranean, all routes to the south and east were routed through West Africa to Khartoum in the Sudan.

During the height of the Battle of Britain in the summer of 1940, BOAC's Empire Boats maintained a transatlantic service for priority passengers and diplomatic mail, with *Clare* making four round trips between Foynes and Botwood from August 3 to September 23, 1940. This route was continued until ice closed Botwood harbor at the end of October. Apart from flying their extensive scheduled routes, the "C" Class 'boats made many unscheduled wartime rescue flights. When Germany invaded Crete, *Coorong* and *Cambria* made 13 round trips between Suda Bay and Alexandria in Egypt, evacuating nearly 500 Allied troops between April 22 and May 5, 1941.

At the end of that year Japan invaded Malaya and Singapore cutting the route to Australia, known as the "Horseshoe Route," and trapping some Empire Boats in the process. Some of these were taken over by QANTAS while several others were pressed into Royal Australian Air Force (RAAF) service. Casualties began to mount.

As the Japanese overran Indonesia at the end of December, *Cassiopeia* crashed on take-off in Sumatra harbor while evacuating BOAC staff and families. Four passengers were killed. On January 31, 1942 *Corio* was shot down by Japanese fighters en route from Darwin to Singapore, killing 13. Twenty were killed three weeks later when *Ceres* was shot down south of Java and, only three days later, *Corinna* was destroyed by Japanese bombers in Broome harbor, Australia. Three other Empire Boats, including the transatlantic veteran *Clare*, were lost in accidents in Africa, while *Maia* was destroyed in Poole harbor during a Luftwaffe night air raid.

BOEINGS FOR BRITAIN

With its aging fleet of Empire Boats taking a heavy toll during wartime operations, BOAC was in desperate need of replacements. Although a few demilitarized RAF Sunderlands and Catalinas were grudgingly released by the Air Ministry to BOAC, they were only stopgaps. Ironically, it would be Imperial Airways' pre-war arch rival Pan American Airways that would provide a solution.

One of the priority passengers who flew to the United States aboard the Empire Boat *Clare* in August 1940 was Lord Balfour, the British government's Under-Secretary of State for Air. His brief was to ask US President Roosevelt for flying training facilities in the USA for British students and to purchase training aircraft for

The most luxurious Flying-Boat in the world
Length 88ft. 6ins. • Height on water line 24ft. • Speed 200 M.P.H. (Approx.)
Span 114 feet • Weight fully loaded 18 tons • Crew 5 - Accommodation 24 passengers on day stages and 16 on night journeys
'The Empire Flying-Boat'-28 are now being built by
IMPERIAL AIRWAYS

LEFT Imperial Airways' "C" Class Empire flying boat was the world's first long-range airliner that rivaled the luxury ocean-going liners of the 1930s with its standard of accommodation, cuisine, and service.

BELOW LEFT An Imperial Airways' poster showing passengers boarding the Empire flying boat Canopus at the airline's quayside seadrome at Southampton in 1937.

the RAF. This having been achieved, Balfour met representatives from military and civil training organizations, including those from the major airlines.

It was in New York that he discovered that Pan Am was considering canceling an order for new advanced versions of its successful pre-war transatlantic flying boat, the Boeing 314. With future commercial flights to Europe in doubt, the airline could only find work on its Pacific routes for three of the six aircraft on order. Balfour met Pan Am's President, Juan Trippe, and a bargain was struck. The Brtish government would pay a net price of £259,250 ($1 million) for each of the Boeings, plus a 5 percent commission for the inspection and acceptance of the boats and the training of the first BOAC air crew. Although Britain was short of dollars and some members of the Government were against the deal, including the Minister of Aircraft Production, Lord Beaverbrook, the first of the Boeing 314As was delivered in June 1941 and put into service on the West Africa and North Atlantic routes. By the end of the year, the Boeings had made 19 round trips across the Atlantic.

The BOAC Boeings, named *Bristol, Berwick,* and *Bangor,* were fitted to carry 44 day passengers or 16 overnight passengers with 11 crew. There were nine cabins: the forward one was for mail, freight, mooring gear, and bunks for the crew, the second was the galley, and the remainder for passengers. Apart from the Lisbon–Lagos route, during summer months flights were made via Botwood to New York and Baltimore. In winter the westbound flights were via Lisbon, Bathurst, Belem in Brazil, Trinidad, and Bermuda, returning via Bermuda, the Azores, and Lisbon.

In January 1942, the British Prime Minister Winston Churchill was flown from Norfolk, Virginia to Bermuda on BOAC Boeing 314A *Berwick,* after meeting President Roosevelt, but on learning of the favorable weather reports he decided to continue across the Atlantic. After flying the 3,365 miles from Bermuda to Poole in 17 hours 55 minutes, Winston Churchill became the first British Prime Minister to make a transatlantic flight. He later flew from Stranraer in Scotland to New York aboard *Bristol* in July 1942.

All three of BOAC's Boeing 314As were still in operation when Germany was defeated. They had flown more than four million

RIGHT BOAC's Boeing 314A *Berwick* seen at Botwood, Canada on the North American leg of the transatlantic route. The flying boat was used by Winston Churchill during a flight from Bermuda to Poole in January 1942.

miles in six years of service carrying VIPs, thousands of passengers, and tons of mail without incident. The type's last transatlantic service was flown by *Berwick*, which left Poole on March 7, 1946 to fly via Bathurst to Baltimore where the 'boats were put up for sale.

Remarkably, after almost 10 years of service, six of which were in punishing war conditions, no less than 13 Empire Boats had survived, the first of which, *Canopus*, had logged over two million miles. As soon as the Japanese surrendered in Burma and Malaya, the "Horseshoe Route" was re-opened with the Empire Boats

flying scheduled services from England to Australia, plus many POW repatriation flights from the Far East.

BOAC's last Empire Boat flights from India and South Africa took place in the spring of 1947, while it was *Coriolanus* that flew the type's last scheduled flight with QANTAS when it flew from Noumea to Rose Bay, Australia on December 20, 1947. All of them were scrapped within a year, although the sole remaining "G" Class 'boat *Golden Hind* languished on the Medway in Kent, England until it was damaged beyond repair in 1954.

Although they had survived the war, commercial flying boats were not able to win the post-war battle against landplanes.

TOP BOAC's first Boeing 314A, named *Bristol*, was delivered to Poole, where it is seen taking off, in June 1941. She carried the British Prime Minister Winston Churchill to New York in July 1942.

BELOW *Cleopatra*, the second long-range S.33 and last of 42 Empire Boats built, arrives over Durban, South Africa on the "Horseshoe Route" in 1944. With a range of 3,300 miles, she went to the breaker's yard in 1946.

BELOW One of three long-range "G" Class Boats, *Golden Hind* uses its outer 1,380hp Bristol Hercules engines to taxi. After serving with the RAF in 1940, she flew the Africa route as a 38-seater and, after the war, flew the Poole to Cairo route until September 1947.

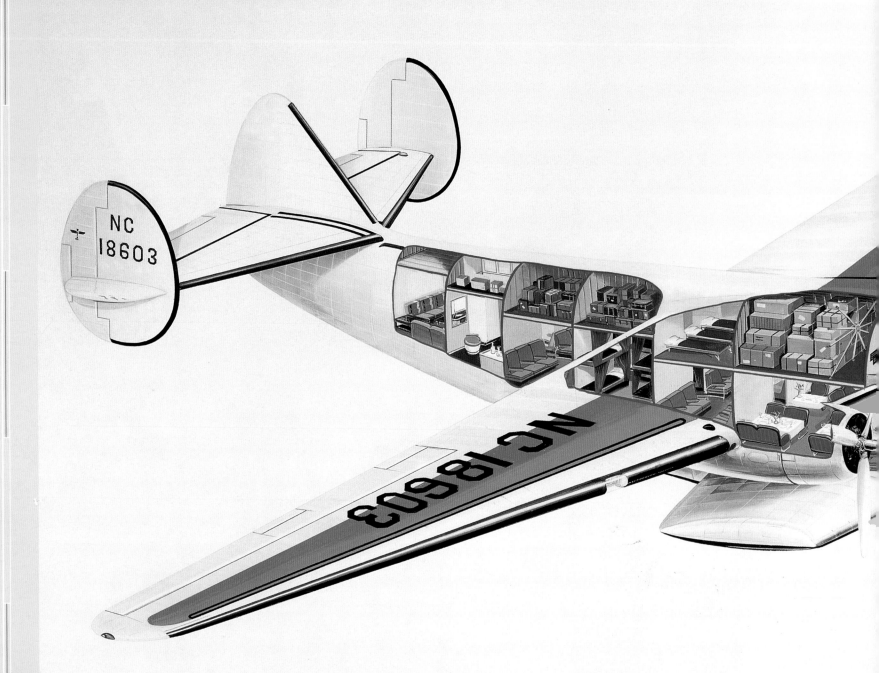

• COTONOU

Juan Trippe was a man with a mission—and that mission was to open up the world to air travel. Born in New Jersey in June 1899 into a well-heeled family (his father was an investment banker), Juan Trippe entered Yale in 1916, where his fellow students included the Vanderbilts, the Whitneys, and the Harrimans, and formed a collegiate flying club in 1917 after learning to fly at the Curtiss Flying School in Miami.

LEFT The largest most luxurious flying boat of its era was the giant Boeing 314 Clipper which flew Pan American Airways first North Atlantic routes in June 1939.

ABOVE The comfortable "dining room" aboard Pan American's first transpacific flying boat, the four-engine Sikorsky S-42.

CONSOLIDATED COMMODORE

Long-range commercial flying boat with a crew of three of the New York, Rio, and Buenos Aires Line (NYRBA) which was taken over by Pan Am in 1930.

STATISTICS

Wingspan	100ft	
Length	68ft	
Height	15ft 8in	
Weight	Empty 10,500lb	Loaded 17,600lb
Engines	Two 575hp Pratt & Whitney Hornet radials	
Max speed	115mph	
Cruise speed	108mph	
Range	1,000 miles	
Passengers	Maximum 32	

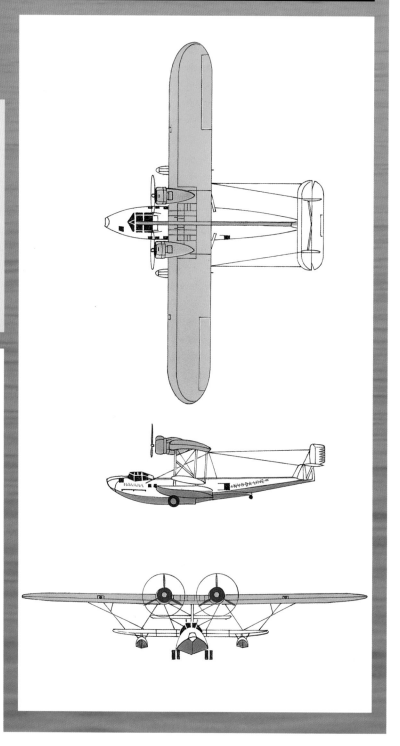

At the end of that year Trippe joined the US Navy and trained as a bomber pilot but saw no action before the war ended. He returned to Yale where he graduated in 1921 and, after a short spell in Wall Street, decided on a career in aviation.

THE BIRTH OF PAN AM

Trippe had been inspired by the formation of Chalk's Flying Service, the first US airline, at Miami in June 1919, and the inauguration of the first American international scheduled passenger air service by Aeromarine West Indies Airways between Key West, Florida and Havana, Cuba in November of that year. He had flown on these embryonic airlines' Curtiss HS-2L flying boats during vacations from Yale and saw the potential of international air travel. Having started a number of unsuccessful air taxi services in New York in the early 1920s, Trippe, backed by some of his wealthy college friends, merged these companies and created a new company called Pan American Airways Inc in 1927.

Using some of his wealthy and influential friends to lobby Washington, Trippe won a contract for his new airline to fly mail to Havana, which he saw as the gateway to South American routes. But Pan Am owned no aircraft and could not afford to purchase any. However, Trippe had the foresight to persuade President Machado of Cuba to grant Pan Am exclusive landing rights in Havana. Armed with this valuable concession, Trippe also managed to convince two other airline bosses who had bid for the Havana contract to merge their companies with his and inject some much-needed funds into the venture.

On October 19, Pan Am finally got into the air flying the 90-mile route between Key West and Havana using a rented Fairchild FC-2 floatplane. For the first few years the airline led a hand-to-

mouth existence but during this period Trippe recruited some of the people who would turn his vision of a global airline into reality. They included a former barnstorming pilot named Edwin C Musick, engineer Andre Priestler, and radio pioneer Hugo Leuteritz. He also widened his circle of influential tycoons, which now included Andrew Mellon, the wealthiest man in Pittsburg and the Secretary of the US Treasury.

In March 1928 the Kelly Foreign Air Mail Act was passed; this authorized private contractors to carry US mail internationally at a rate of two dollars per pound per mile. A few weeks later, Trippe, with a little help from his friends, won two international routes—one to Trinidad via Cuba and Puerto Rico, and the other from Cuba to Panama via Mexico. In order to capitalize on these routes Trippe formed a close relationship with Igor Sikorsky and ordered the first of a series of his amphibious flying boat designs, the S-38. He also bought out his only competitor on the Cuba to Trinidad route, the West Indian Aerial Express.

ABOVE AND BELOW LEFT
The first flying boat designed by Igor Sikorsky to be operated by Pan American Airways was the S-38, a 10-passenger amphibian used on local routes from Miami in 1929.

TOP Twin-engine all-metal Consolidated Commodore long-range flying boats which carried 32 passengers were built for NYRBA's Miami to the Argentine route in 1929, but were taken over by Pan Am a year later.

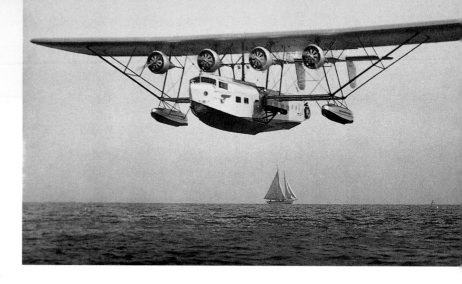

Although the United States government had no financial investment in any airline, it preferred to deal with one strong airline that could rival state-backed overseas airlines such as France's Aeropostale—later Air France—Germany's Lufthansa, and Great Britain's Imperial Airways, and that airline was Pan American. By the early 1930s, Pan Am had been awarded several other overseas contracts and Trippe's airline could be assured of some $50 million in mail revenues over the next 20 years. He could now take on the world. First, he hired America's transatlantic hero, Charles Lindbergh, as Pan Am technical adviser, and in 1930 Trippe made another important acquisition, the New York, Rio, and Buenos Aires Line Inc, known as NYRBA.

Founded by World War One "ace" Ralph O'Neill, NYRBA had established regular flights between Miami and Buenos Aires via the West Indies, Uruguay, and Brazil, a route of almost 9,000 miles covered in seven days. To operate this route, the airline had invested heavily in a fleet of 14 luxurious 20-passenger Consolidated Commodore flying boats. Powered by two 575hp Pratt & Whitney Hornet radial engines and resembling a large Dornier Wal, the all-metal Commodore cruised at a sedate 108mph over a range of 1,000 miles. Although the route proved highly successful, the cost of the Consolidated 'boats and the effects of the Wall Street crash caused NYRBA to lose money, forcing its backers to sell out to Pan Am.

BELOW LEFT The 32-passenger four-engine Sikorsky S-42 was one of Pan Am's most famous flying boats, carrying out the first Pacific and North Atlantic survey flights in 1935 and 1937.

ABOVE Pan American Airways' first Clippers were the four-engine Sikorsky S-40 amphibious flying boats, three of which entered service in 1931 carrying 32 passengers on the Miami to Panama Canal Zone route.

PAN AM GOES FROM STRENGTH TO STRENGTH

Trippe now ran an international airline flying more than 20,000 miles to 20 countries, but that was only the beginning. Pan Am aircrews all wore smart naval-type uniforms and the US government used the airline whenever it was flying government officials, evacuating US citizens in time of crisis, or sending humanitarian aid to countries in South and Central America hit by natural disaster. Pan Am was America's "official" airline. In 1931, the first of the famed Pan Am Flying Clippers, the Sikorsky S-40, was introduced into service. Powered by four Hornet engines, the amphibians could accommodate 32 passengers and flew the 600-mile Jamaica to Panama sector of the South American route, which, at the time, constituted the world's longest scheduled air flight.

But Trippe now had his sights on the Pacific and Atlantic routes and risked all by ordering a fleet of 10 advanced long-range Sikorsky S-42 flying boats in 1932. Making its first flight in March 1934, the 32-seat S-42 powered by four 700hp Hornets had a range of over 1,200 miles and entered service on the Miami to Rio de Janeiro route in August 1934. Trippe wanted the S-42 to fly the Pacific route, the first sector of which would be the 2,400 miles from California to Hawaii. First tested by Charles Lindbergh, the S-42 could reach Hawaii but with no useful payload and no margins. Therefore, a more powerful version of the Sikorsky flying boat was ordered, the S-42B fitted with uprated engines and extra fuel tanks.

It was the first of these 'boats, named *Pan American Clipper*,

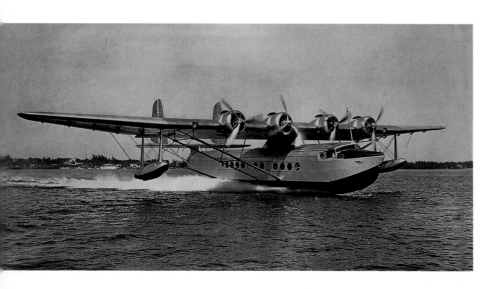

that was flown by Edwin Musick and a crew of five on a route survey flight from Alameda Airport in San Francisco Bay, the airline's new West Coast base, to Hawaii in April 1935. By this time, the first of three giant Martin 130 flying boats—powered by four 950hp Pratt & Whitney Twin Wasp engines which gave it a cruising speed of 160mph and a maximum range of almost 4,000 miles, ordered by Pan Am off the drawing board in 1933 at a cost of $417,000 each—had made its maiden flight. It was the first of these, appropriately named *China Clipper*, that took off from San Francisco Bay on November 22, 1935 at the start of the first airmail flight across the Pacific, with pilot Edwin Musick at the aircraft's controls.

After making refueling stops at Hawaii, Midway Island, Wake Island, and Guam, *China Clipper* touched down in Manila harbor in the Philippines on November 29. The 8,210-mile route was completed in a few minutes under 60 hours flying time, spread over six-and-a-half days. To ensure that the transpacific flight would succeed, Pan Am invested $1 million in en route facilities. The airline's chief engineer Andre Priestler built bases, hotels, and crew quarters on each of the island stopovers and an impressive flying boat terminus in Manila. An advanced communications and navigation system was created by Hugo Leuteritz, with radio masts and communications cabins being erected along the Clipper routes. Moreover, prior to the *China Clipper*'s first flight, Musick had surveyed the route in the S-42 *Pan American Clipper*. Trippe had planned for the transpacific flights to terminate at Hong Kong

but the British government refused to grant landing rights until Trippe had successfully negotiated landing rights in neighboring Macao with the Portuguese.

With the prospect of US tourists being able to fly to Hawaii, Pan Am concluded an agreement with a local airline, Inter-Island Airways, formed in January 1929 using four S-38C amphibians, to fly Pan Am passengers on its inter-island services from October 1936. Inter-Island, later renamed Hawaiian Airlines, subsequently ordered four S-43 Baby Clippers to cope with the additional traffic.

ABOVE Pan Am's Martin 130 *China Clipper* flying over San Francisco's unfinished Golden Gate Bridge, leaving on its inaugural mail flight across the Pacific on November 22, 1935.

BELOW A cutaway of a Pan Am Sikorsky S-42 showing the four passenger compartments each with eight seats, the galley and the four-crew flight deck.

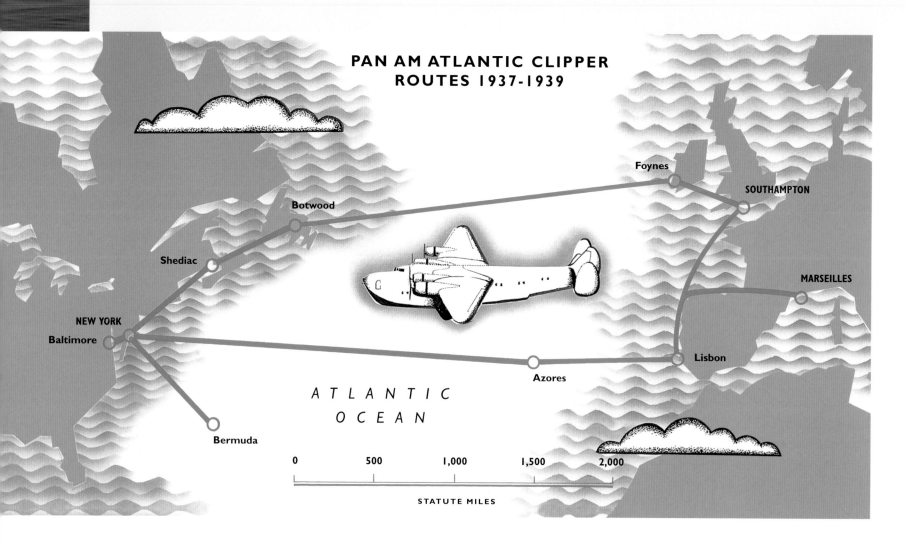

PAN AM ATLANTIC CLIPPER ROUTES 1937-1939

Foynes

SOUTHAMPTON

Botwood

MARSEILLES

Shediac

NEW YORK

Baltimore

Lisbon

Azores

ATLANTIC OCEAN

Bermuda

| 0 | 500 | 1,000 | 1,500 | 2,000 |

STATUTE MILES

ACROSS THE OCEANS

On October 21, 1936, Pan Am inaugurated the first transpacific passenger service. The maximum seating on the 130-foot wingspan Martin 130s was 41, but on the transpacific route only 14 were carried. Only seven passengers boarded the first flight to Manila, each paying $1,438 for the round trip and almost the same again if they continued to Hong Kong on an S-42. On this inaugural flight, the number of passengers equaled the number of crew who would cater to their every wish. Food and cabin accommodation were on a par with that of luxury liners of the day, as were the Pan Am hotels en route. Having succeeded in establishing the first commercial transpacific route, which in 1937 was extended to New Zealand, the North Atlantic was Trippe's next proposed conquest.

On July 5, 1937 S-42B *Clipper III* flew Pan Am's first North Atlantic survey flight when it flew from New York to Foynes, Ireland via the Azores and Lisbon. To fly the airline's North

TOP Pan Am Boeing 314 *Clipper* flying boats were the first commercial aircraft to fly regular scheduled non-stop flights across the North Atlantic.

ABOVE *Hawaii Clipper*, moored at Pan Am's west coast terminal at San Francisco, the third and last Martin 130 delivered to Pan Am in 1935, was lost with all on board after leaving Guam in June 1938.

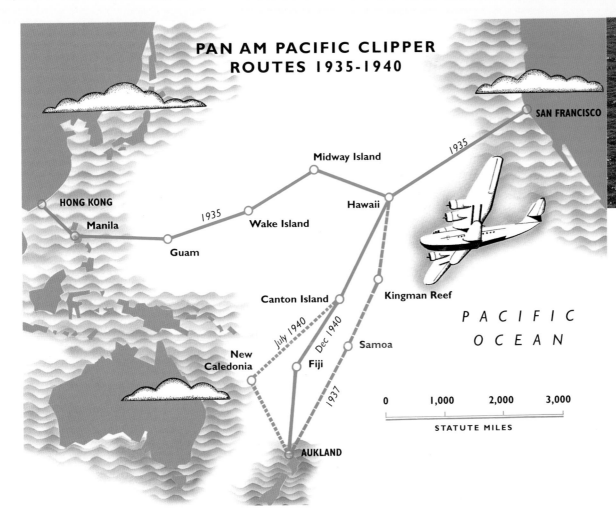

PAN AM PACIFIC CLIPPER ROUTES 1935-1940

SAN FRANCISCO

Midway Island

HONG KONG

Manila

1935

Wake Island

Hawaii

Guam

Canton Island

Kingman Reef

July 1940

Dec 1940

Samoa

New Caledonia

Fiji

1937

PACIFIC OCEAN

0   1,000   2,000   3,000

STATUTE MILES

AUKLAND

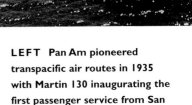

LEFT Pan Am pioneered transpacific air routes in 1935 with Martin 130 inaugurating the first passenger service from San Francisco to Manila in October 1936.

ABOVE The Martin 130 *China Clipper* seen on its take-off run across San Francisco Bay at the start of a flight to Hawaii, the first leg of Pan Am's transpacific route to Manila in the Philippines.

BELOW An artist captures the dramatic arrival in the Orient of Pan Am's Martin 130 *China Clipper* on its inaugural flight across the Pacific ocean in 1935.

Atlantic service, Trippe had ordered the "jumbo jet" of flying boats, the Boeing 314. Powered by four 1,600hp Wright Cyclone GR-2000 engines, it had a crew of 10 and could carry up to 74 day passengers or 40 with sleeping berths at a cruising speed of 188mph over a maximum range of 3,685 miles. Pan Am's first Boeing 314, named *Dixie Clipper*, flew in June 1938 and began the airline's first scheduled airmail service over the North Atlantic on May 20, 1939. At the same time, the newly formed American Export Airlines applied for a license to operate a regular flying boat passenger service over the route using Vought–Sikorsky VS-44As, and Trippe resorted once again to his loyal band of governmental lobbyists and won the day.

However, the airline had suffered two major setbacks in the Pacific. On January 11, 1938 Edwin Musick, piloting the S-42B *Samoan Clipper* and taking off from Pago Pago harbor in US Samoa en route to New Zealand, was lost with his crew when the Sikorsky exploded following a fuel leak. Six months later the

RIGHT Pan Am bought 14 Sikorsky S-43 Baby Clippers for its operations in Brazil in 1936. The type was also used by Hawaii's Inter-Island Airways and by the French airline Aeromaritime in West Africa.

BELOW *Dixie Clipper* was the first Boeing 314 flying boat to be delivered to Pan Am and the first to fly a regular non-stop North Atlantic service on June 28, 1939.

a fleet of 14 Sikorsky S-43 Baby Clippers for use in Brazil and on the Seattle to Alaska routes, were mounting and on March 14, 1939 he was replaced as Pan Am chief executive by the airline's largest stockholder, Sonny Whitney. After nine months of inertia, Trippe was back in charge but, with Europe on the brink of war, Pan Am's future was about to change out of all recognition.

It seems ironic that the golden age of the flying boat, when huge luxury liners of the skies were operated by the likes of Imperial Airways and Pan Am, came about during a time of worldwide economic depression. However, Trippe in particular knew that bolstered by lucrative mail contracts, there would always be enough people who could afford to fly first class on his airline—bankers, film stars, gangsters, and government officials—despite stock market crashes and political turmoil. Pan Am was also able to command very competitive prices from aircraft manufacturers desperate for contracts during this period.

By June 1939, three of Pan Am's six Boeing 314s were flying non-stop services from New York to Lisbon, a flight time of 25 hours, while the others operated on the Pacific routes and another six improved 314A Clippers were on order.

THE IMPACT OF WAR

Britain's declaration of war on Germany in September, 1939 was a mixed blessing for Pan American Airways. Its South American and Pacific routes were initially unaffected while demand for its transatlantic routes quadrupled overnight. The Clipper service to neutral Portugal was in demand from politicians, arms dealers, and refugees from almost every country in Europe, and with every German victory this traffic increased. The downside was that Pan Am now had competition on the North Atlantic routes, from BOAC Empire Boats and, from July 1940, from American Export Airlines' postponed VS-44A service.

In fact, BOAC was so desperate to increase its transatlantic operations that it negotiated a deal with Trippe whereby three of the 314A Clippers were purchased by the British airline in 1941. One of the remaining three new Boeings, *Capetown Clipper*, was bought by the US government in August 1941 and leased back to

M-130 *Hawaiian Clipper* crashed into the sea between Guam and Manila killing six passengers and nine crew. With the New Zealand route suspended and passenger confidence in the Martin flying boats severely reduced, the Pacific route began to lose money. Debts incurred by Trippe, who had heavily committed the airline to a program of global expansion which included the purchase of

Pan Am to operate a ferrying and transport service for the United States government over the South Atlantic across Africa and over to the Middle East.

The Japanese attack on Pearl Harbor on December 7, 1941 brought the golden age of the Pacific Clippers to an end. The Martin 130 *Philippine Clipper* was caught at Wake Island and damaged by a Japanese air raid which killed nine Pan Am employees. The following day, the S-42B *Hong Kong Clipper II*, which flew the Manila–Hong Kong–Macao route, was sunk at its moorings at Kai Tak Airport in Kowloon by Japanese bombers.

LEFT *Yankee Clipper*, seen here taking off from Botswood, Newfoundland, was the second Boeing 314 to fly the North Atlantic route after delivery in 1939.

BELOW Pan Am's third Boeing 314, *American Clipper* powers its way off the water in New York harbor en route for Lisbon, Portugal prior to the outbreak of war in Europe.

ABOVE One of three Pan Am Boeing Clippers that took over the Pacific route from the Martin 130s at the end of 1939, seen approaching the completed Golden Gate Bridge homeward-bound from Hawaii.

On the same day Boeing 314 *Pacific Clipper* was on the last leg of its four-day flight from San Francisco to Auckland, New Zealand with 21 passengers and a crew of 10. Its scheduled return route was now cut by the invading Japanese and its only way back would be to fly westward.

On December 15, New York ordered the *Pacific Clipper* to take off for Australia then fly northwest to the Dutch West Indies, Ceylon, India, Bahrain, Sudan, and to the Belgian Congo. The flight from Leopoldville, in the Congo, to Natal in Brazil took 24 hours 35 minutes, but the flight to Trinidad and on to New York where *Pacific Clipper* touched down on January 6, 1942 was the easy bit.

Capt Bob Ford and his crew had flown more than 31,500 miles to complete the first round-the-world flight by a commercial aircraft. The epic flight had been completed in 209 flying hours over unfamiliar routes often using only an atlas for navigation, with fuel shortages, one engine failure, and practically no direct communication with the outside world.

A CLOSE SHAVE

During 1942, Pan Am established its regular wartime schedules carrying mainly military personnel and high-priority civilians on restricted passenger services over both the Pacific and the Atlantic. What follows is an extract from a description of a typical wartime flight from New York to Southampton from a junior pilot, and later a Pan Am Boeing 747 Captain, Roger Sherron:

"After serving in the Communications Department, first as a radio mechanic and later as a flight radio officer, I obtained my

commercial pilot's license and was hired as a junior pilot in the spring of 1941.

Normal pilot progression in those days on the Boeing 314 Clippers was to start as a fourth officer (relief pilot), then serve as a third officer, again a relief pilot, second officer (navigation after qualifying), and first officer (in temporary command after qualifying in aircraft handling, while the captain rested). Included in the operating crew were two radio operators and two flight engineers. This gave us the equivalent of two complete crews and our duty times were not limited. At the time we were the only air link between North America and Europe, a service which was considered essential by the United States government. Three Boeing 314As were purchased by BOAC and they had begun flying scheduled transatlantic services in 1941.

Pan American had two original transatlantic routes, the first being New York–Bermuda–Horta, Azores–Lisbon,

ABOVE The lower-deck dining room of a pre-war Pan Am Boeing 314 Clipper could seat 12 at a sitting, with passengers eating a six-course meal from bone china crockery with bowls of fresh roses in the window.

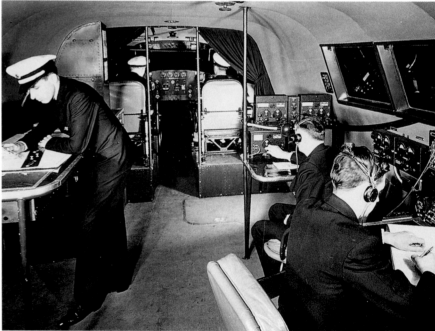

ABOVE A view of the Boeing 314's spacious flight deck looking forward with the navigator's chart table on the left and the radio operator's station on the right.

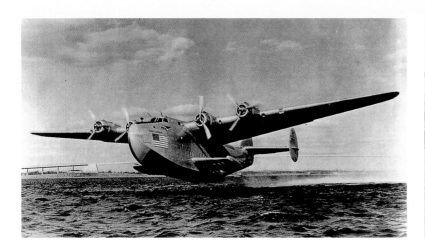

ABOVE A heavily loaded *Yankee Clipper* lifts off from San Francisco Bay at the start of a transpacific flight to Hong Kong in early 1941. Note the Boeing 314's Dornier-style sponsons and lack of wingtip floats.

ABOVE *Pacific Clipper*, which made the first round-the-world flight after the Japanese attack on Pearl Harbor in December 1941, moored at San Francisco flying a windswept "star and stripes."

Portugal–Marseilles, France, and the other, known as the North Atlantic route, was New York–Shediec, New Brunswick–Botwood, Newfoundland–Foynes, Ireland–Southampton. Due to hostilities in Europe, the legs from Lisbon to Marseilles, and later Foynes to Southampton were dropped. Also, because of westerly winds which caused limited payloads on westbound flights especially in winter, the whole north route was eventually dropped. Flights to Lisbon were continued on to Foynes as this provided an important link between the United States and the United Kingdom. We continued to provide this service until the end of World War Two.

On October 30, 1942 I departed New York aboard *Yankee Clipper* bound for Foynes by way of Bermuda, Horta, and Lisbon, with Captain C R Titus in command. I had been moved up to first officer, but this was my first transatlantic flight as such. Due to weather and ocean surface conditions at Horta, delays and changes occurred, and we departed Horta on November 5 on *Atlantic Clipper* bound for Lisbon.

The first part of the flight was routine, above broken cloud layers at about 8,000 feet with pilots changing seats for rest and meal breaks. In the latter part of the 13-hour flight, Capt Titus was seated in the left-hand pilot's seat, with me in the right-hand one. We had been flying in and out of cloud with occasional glimpses of the ocean below. Conditions changed and we came out of the cloud into what looked like beautiful weather ahead. Then we saw the convoy! The ocean below was filled with ships.

Our pre-flight briefing had covered a number of items including the strict instruction never to fly over a convoy or an assembly of ships. Also included were recognition signals for the day identifying us as friendly to any Allied forces we might encounter. The Very pistol used for firing the recognition colors was at my side. Capt Titus remarked that it was probably too late to change course at this stage and ordered me to fire the recognition signal. I opened the side window of the cockpit, pointed the Very pistol in front of and above the number three and four propellers and fired the proper recognition signal.

At almost the same time, an anti-aircraft burst was observed ahead and below. The Captain ordered me to fire another recognition signal, which I did post haste. Almost immediately, it seemed that every gunner in the convoy followed the lead of the first one and black puffs below us rapidly increased in number and they were getting uncomfortably close. At this point, Capt Titus had had more than enough. He quickly took the aircraft off autopilot, made a steep turn to reverse our course, and headed for the clouds. We stayed on the reverse course until we were well clear of the convoy. Then, having noted that the ships were on a more or less southerly course, we flew north a sufficient distance to clear the convoy and any of its wide-ranging escorts. Only then did we resume our heading towards Lisbon.

On debriefing, we were advised that we must have been mistaken, no such thing had happened and that we best forget what we had seen and above all, say nothing!

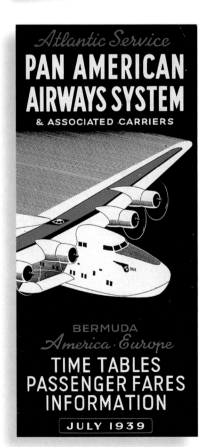

LEFT The colorful Pan Am timetable of routes to Nassau, the West Indies, and South America operated by Sikorsky S.42s.

BELOW LEFT The timetable of Pan Am's pioneering North Atlantic passenger routes flown by Boeing 314 Clippers in July 1939.

BELOW *American Clipper* moored off Pan Am's New York terminal displaying a prominent "stars and stripes" on the nose, which was adopted in 1940 after the outbreak of war in Europe.

Some time later we heard news of Operation *Torch*, the Allied landings in North Africa and then realized what we had stumbled across, and how lucky we were not to have been shot down by our own forces. Part of our luck was the hasty and inaccurate shooting by the anti-aircraft gunners aided by the probability that this was the first time they had fired shots in anger!

The amphibious assaults at Casablanca, Oran, and Algiers by US and British task forces took place on November 8, 1942. Three naval task forces departed the east coast of the United States from different ports, assembled in mid-Atlantic and then proceeded to the beaches of North Africa. We had the misfortune to pop out of the cloud cover right over the whole lot!

We made our trip to Foynes and back to Lisbon, but because of weather and other conditions, the flight from Lisbon to New York was made by way of the west coast of Africa and east coast of South America. Uneventful."

None of the Pan Am Boeing Clippers were lost during their six years of continuous operations over the world's longest sea routes. The Martin 130s did not survive the war. The *Philippine Clipper*

crashed into a mountain while flying over northern California in 1943 and the original *China Clipper* struck a submerged obstacle while landing at Trinidad on January 8, 1945. Twelve passengers and nine members of the crew were killed. Four of Pan Am's S-42s were still active at the end of the war but they were scrapped soon after. Two of the larger Sikorsky VS-44As of Pan Am's rival, American Export Airlines, made 405 Atlantic crossings between January 1942 and October 1945 when they were retired. One VS-44A crashed on take-off in October 1942.

When the war ended, so did the dominance of the great flying boats. Modern airfields and navigation aids were now available all over the world, and modern transport aircraft, developed for the military, could carry more passengers over greater distances than many of the pre-war big 'boats. Their time was nearly over.

TOP LEFT High priority passengers disembarking from Boeing 314 *Dixie Clipper* at Pan Am's east coast terminal after a wartime North Atlantic crossing from Lisbon.

TOP RIGHT Passengers boarding a Pan Am Sikorsky S.42 at its Miami, Florida flying boat terminal.

CENTER RIGHT Pan Am's US monopoly of the North Atlantic route came to an end in 1940 when American Export Airlines began flying from New York to Lisbon with 16 passenger Vought-Sikorsky VS-44A flying boats.

RIGHT Boeing 314A *Capetown Clipper* in its wartime camouflage was bought by the US government in 1941 and leased to Pan Am to operate a service to the Middle East via the South Atlantic.

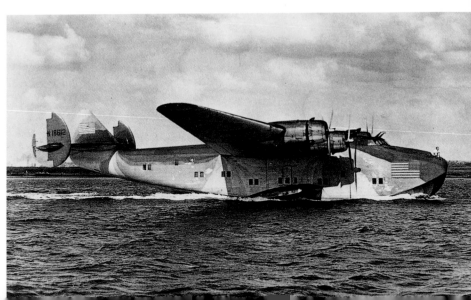

The outbreak of World War Two in September 1939 saw the flying boat holding a dominant position in civil aviation. The new generation of all-metal, multi-engine monoplane commercial flying boats designed in the 1930s for Pan American, Imperial Airways, and Lufthansa were far more advanced than many military 'boats of the same era, which tended to be updated reincarnations of World War One Curtiss and Felixstowe designs.

LEFT A small Grumman amphibian, the Widgeon, was extensively used by the Allies for air-sea rescue and coastal patrol duties, with a US Coast Guard J4F-1 sinking a U-boat in the Gulf of Mexico, 1942.

ABOVE At the outbreak of World War Two, RAF and RCAF squadrons were still equipped with biplane Supermarine Stranraer II flying boats. The type's last wartime patrol was flown with 240 Squadron in March 1941.

CONSOLIDATED PBY-5 CATALINA

A version of the world's most successful flying boat, the long-range maritime reconnaissance flying boat with a crew of seven to nine, built by Naval Aircraft Factory, the PBN-1 Nomad was operated by the US Navy and RAAF.

STATISTICS

Wingspan	104ft
Length	65ft 13in
Height	20ft 2in
Weight	Empty 20,100lb Loaded 35,420lb
Engines	Two 1,200hp Pratt & Whitney R-1830 radials
Max speed	179mph
Cruise speed	103mph
Range	2,760 miles
Armament	2x.303in and 2x.50in Browning machine guns 4,000lb bombload

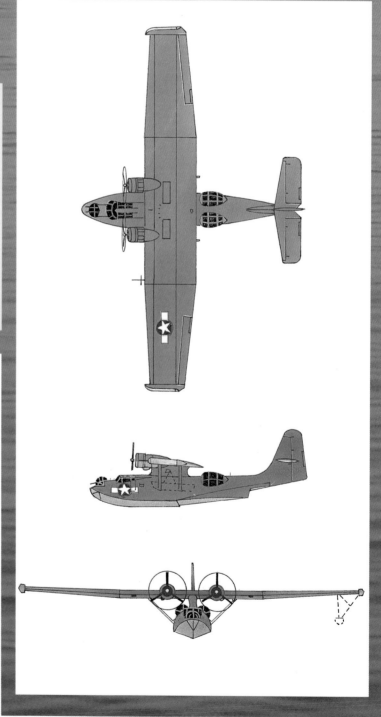

The most successful flying boat of World War Two, which not only saw the widest service but which would be produced in larger numbers than any other flying boat in the world, was developed from the Commodore 16 long-range commercial transport and the P2Y military variant. The first P3Y, a twin-engine parasol-wing flying boat designed by the Consolidated Aircraft Corporation of New York, flew for the first time in March 1935 and established a new world seaplane distance record flying from Norfolk, Virginia non-stop to the Panama Canal Zone—a distance of 3,190 miles. The first production boats, re-designated the PBY-1, were delivered to US Navy Squadron VP-11F in October 1936 and the remarkable military career of this flying boat had begun. During the next two years, the Soviet Union became the first export customer for the PBY-3, closely followed by the British Air Ministry which purchased a single example for evaluation early in 1939.

THE OPENING SKIRMISHES

Three years later, RAF and Luftwaffe flying boats were in action within hours of the outbreak of war in Europe. Although the RAF had a number of 1930s vintage Short Rangoon and Supermarine Stranraer biplane flying boats in service, it was the RAF's most famous flying boat, the Short Sunderland, developed from the Empire Boats, that replaced them. First flown in October 1937, the long-range maritime reconnaissance flying boat powered by four 1,010hp Bristol Pegasus engines carried a crew of 13 and equipped three Coastal Command squadrons by September 1939. The Sunderland I, armed with seven .303in machine guns, could carry a 2,000lb bombload suspended on railed racks wound out of the interior of the hull under the wings, and was equipped with sleeping berths, a galley, and a well-equipped workshop. Flying at 200mph, it had an endurance of 12 hours. The type carried out its first wartime rescue on September 18 when two Sunderlands of 204 and 228 Squadrons picked up 34 crew of a torpedoed merchant ship, the *Kensington Court*, off the Scillies.

Ten days later, a flying boat became the first Luftwaffe aircraft to be shot down by British fighters. One of three Dornier Do 18Ds, the military version of the Do 18V developed from the Wal as a transatlantic mail carrier, was shot down over the North Sea on September 29 by Fleet Air Arm Skuas from the carrier HMS *Ark Royal*. Another Do 18G on a reconnaissance mission over Jutland became the first victim of an RAF fighter when it was shot down by a Hudson of 224 Squadron based at RAF Leuchars in Scotland on October 8.

Although this period was known as the Phoney War, German U-boats operated virtually unchecked, wreaking havoc against British shipping in the western approaches from the first day of hostilities. Despite Coastal Command Sunderlands making numerous sightings during the first months of war, it came as a relief when a 228 Squadron flying boat sunk U-55 on January 31, 1940, although bad weather over the Atlantic and the North Sea hampered more attacks on enemy shipping until the end of March. On April 3, a 204 Squadron Sunderland was attacked by no less than six Ju 88s but, although hit several times, the

TOP Developed for the Netherlands in 1938, versions of the Do 24 built in Holland, France, and Germany served with Luftwaffe flying boat units in air-sea rescue and transport roles from Norway to Greece.

ABOVE The first Luftwaffe aircraft shot down by British fighters in 1939 was the Dornier Do 18 flying boat, developed from this pre-war Lufthansa transatlantic mail plane.

Sunderland managed to fight off its attackers downing at least one in the process and seriously damaging a second, to land safely at Invergordon in Scotland.

It was RAF Sunderlands of the same squadron that confirmed that Norway would be Germany's next target when the flying boats located a German battle fleet led by the cruiser *Hipper* on April 8–9 heading for Trondheim. During the early days of the German invasion of Norway, six former Lufthansa Dornier Do 26 flying boats powered by four 700hp Jumo diesel engines were used by the Luftwaffe for transporting 10 to 12 fully equipped troops into Narvik Bay. On May 28, RAF Hurricanes of 46 Squadron attacked two of them disembarking alpine troops in Rombaksfjord, setting them both on fire. During May and June, Royal Navy Supermarine Walrus ship-spotting amphibians, known in naval circles as the "Shagbat," of 710 Squadron carried by six British warships sent to Norway were used to strafe enemy positions, fly anti-submarine patrols, and ferry troops ashore. One of the single-engine biplane flying boats, descendants of R J Mitchell's 1922 Seagull I, was shot down by a Luftwaffe He 111, while the rest were evacuated with the British Expeditionary Force (BEF) at the beginning of June 1, 1940.

As the Battle of France drew to a close, a 10 Squadron Sunderland was sent on a secret mission to North Africa. On June 25, it took off from Calshot carrying Lord Gort VC, the Commander-in-Chief of the BEF in France, and Duff Cooper, British Minister of Information, for the flight to Rabat in French Morocco. After a hazardous landing on a narrow river among native boats at dusk, the VIPs met a number of high-ranking French officials who had fled from France to try and secure Free French cooperation in North Africa. The mission almost failed when the local police chief attempted to arrest the Sunderland crew, but early the next morning the flying boat and its distinguished passengers took off for Calshot via Gibraltar, where Lord Gort and Duff Cooper disembarked. Soon after, the Walrus became part of Britain's first air-sea rescue organisation hastily established during the Battle of Britain which began on July 10, 1940. The Luftwaffe already had an efficient air-sea rescue service using Heinkel He 59 floatplanes which flew over the Channel unmolested until it was discovered that they were using long-range radio equipment to direct formations of German bombers to British convoys and coastal targets. Several were subsequently shot down by RAF fighters during the four-month battle.

OPPOSITE TOP One of the initial export customers for the Consolidated PBY-3 Catalina was the Soviet Union, which put the type in production at Taganrog in 1939. More than a hundred served with the Soviet Navy.

LEFT Originally ordered for the RAAF, the Supermarine Walrus served throughout the war in all theaters as a fleet-spotter, light bomber, and air-sea rescue amphibian with the Royal Navy, RAF, RAAF, and RNZAF.

BELOW The only flying boat of Russian design operated by the Soviet Navy during the war was the five-man short-range Beriev MBR-2 reconnaissance aircraft, more than 1,500 of which were built between 1931 and 1942.

WAR IN THE MEDITERRANEAN

By June 10, Italy had entered the war and 228 Squadron moved to Malta and Alexandria, from where one of its Sunderlands sank the first Italian submarine in the Mediterranean. The following day the same 'boat sank a second Italian submarine, the *Rubino*, landed and picked up its crew, and attacked yet another submarine en route to Malta. When fighting broke out in Somaliland in July, Royal Navy Walruses from HMS *Dorsetshire*, *Hobart*, and *Leander* were used as light bombers against Italian forces and later in the year, *Dorsetshire*'s amphibian stalked the Vichy French battleship *Richelieu* off Dakar. In November, a 228 Squadron Sunderland flew from Malta to carry out vital reconnaissance at Taranto prior to the Fleet Air Arm's crippling attack there on the Italian fleet.

After a slow start, RAF Sunderland successes against the formidable U-boat began to mount with one 204 Squadron flying boat named *Queen of the Air* by its captain Flt Lt Ernest Baker sinking four submarines between August 16 and December 6, 1940 in the North Atlantic. To supplement Coastal Command's sub-hunting fleet, the first of more than 600 Consolidated PBY-5 long-range flying boats, named Catalina Is, were delivered to the RAF in early 1941. Issued to 209 and 240 Squadrons based in the Shetlands, they soon proved their value by spotting and shadowing the German battleship *Bismark* on May 26 after it had eluded Royal Navy warships.

Earlier that month, RAF flying boats were heavily engaged in the evacuation of Commonwealth troops from Greece and Crete after Germany's victorious Greek campaign. Six Sunderlands of

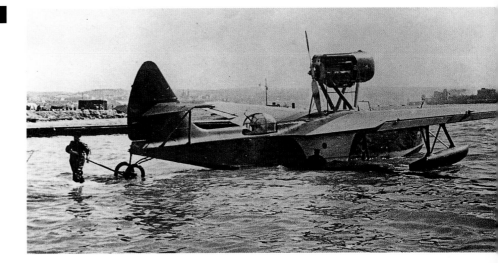

228 and 230 Squadrons flew 782 people, including King George II of Greece and members of the royal family, from Greece to Crete between April 20 and 27. Three hundred fourteen were then flown on to Alexandria. One 228 Squadron boat carried a record passenger load of 84.

Later that year, the largest flying boat to see operational service in World War Two made a series of record-breaking flights to and from Greece. The Luftwaffe's Blohm und Voss Bv 222 Viking had been designed for Lufthansa's transatlantic services. It was powered by six 1,200hp BMW Bramo engines, had a wingspan of 150 feet, and could carry up to 92 fully equipped troops. In October 1941 the prototype Viking, which had made its maiden flight almost exactly a year earlier, made 17 flights between Athens and Derna in Libya, carrying supplies for German forces into Greece and evacuating a total of 515 casualties.

THE WAR SPREADS

On December 7, 1941 the whole complexion of the war changed with the Japanese attack on the US Navy at Pearl Harbor, Hawaii. In addition to the 18 warships sunk by Japanese carrier aircraft, nearly 200 US aircraft were destroyed including many US Navy seaplanes and flying boats. On the same day, RAF Catalinas of 205 Squadron based at Seletar in Singapore shadowed a Japanese battle fleet off Siam (Thailand), and one was shot down by Japanese fighters. By the end of 1941 the first of 169 Royal Australian Air Force Catalinas were becoming operational with the newly formed 11 and 20 Squadrons, which became part of the joint Australian–British–Dutch–American (ABDA) Command, along with the three US Navy PBY-5 units, VP-101, VP-102, and VP-22 of Patrol Wing 10 based in Australia.

In the Atlantic, the US Navy had been operating neutrality convoy patrols from Newfoundland and Iceland with PBY-5s since May 1941, and these were joined by Martin PBM-1 Mariners at Norfolk, Virginia. Soon after completing the successful Martin 130 Pacific Clippers for Pan Am and a much larger development, the M-156 sold to the Soviet Union in 1938 and used as a naval transport during the war, the Glenn L Martin Company designed a twin-engine gull-wing maritime reconnaissance flying boat which entered service with the US Navy in late 1940. The Mariner

RIGHT Almost as many Catalinas, such as this 210 Squadron flying boat, as Sunderlands served with RAF Coastal Command and overseas squadrons from 1941 to 1945 as U-boat killers.

BELOW LEFT Ford Island Naval Air Station at Pearl Harbor, Hawaii seen during the Japanese air raid on December 7, 1941 with a shattered Catalina wing lying in the foreground and a damaged flying boat in the background.

was the first US Navy flying boat to sink a U-boat when U-153 was caught on the surface in the Caribbean in July 1942.

By this time a new variant of the Sunderland, with a re-designed planing hull and fitted with air to surface vessel (ASV) radar was being delivered to RAF and RAAF squadrons. U-boat sinkings in the North Atlantic now gathered momentum. On July 31, U-754 was sunk by a Royal Canadian Air Force (RCAF) Catalina off Nova Scotia, while only two days later U-166 was destroyed by a US Coast Guard Widgeon of 212 Squadron off the Mississippi River basin. The small twin-engine three to five-seat Grumman Widgeon was designed before the war as a "millionaire's yacht," as was its stablemate the Grumman Goose; both of these were adopted by the military and served with the US Navy and Coast Guard, the RAF, and the Royal Navy in coastal patrol, air-sea rescue, training, and communications roles throughout the war.

During 1942 large convoys of war materials sailing from Scotland to Murmansk in the Soviet Union were prime targets for U-boats. Norway-based Blohm und Voss Bv 138 long-range flying boats were given the task of shadowing the convoys. In June a Walrus from HMS *Norfolk* escorting convoy PQ17 was attacked by a three-engine twin-boom Bv 138, one of the few instances of air

combat between two flying boats, and was forced down on the North Atlantic where it was taken in tow by a merchant ship. Both the Walrus and its crew were lucky to be rescued by one of the few ships of PQ17 that managed to reach Murmansk. In September, the next convoy, PQ18, was also sighted by Luftwaffe Bv 138s which often refueled from U-boats at sea, but this time they were chased away by Fleet Air Arm Sea Hurricanes from one of the escort carriers.

On August 25, 228 Squadron, one of the original and most experienced Sunderland units, suffered a tragedy when one of its flying boats carrying the Duke of Kent from Invergordon to Iceland crashed into high ground near Caithness, soon after take-off. All on board, except the rear gunner, were killed in the accident. However, by the end of 1942 more than a dozen U-boats had been destroyed in the Atlantic by Catalina and Sunderland flying boats.

TOP LEFT Six Royal Netherlands Naval Air Service Do 24K flying boats managed to escape from the Dutch East Indies when the Japanese invaded in 1942, and were impressed into the RAAF's 41 Squadron.

TOP RIGHT More than 350 Grumman Goose amphibians were produced for the US Navy, Coast Guard, and Army Air Force, RAF (seen here), and RCAF for coastal patrol, navigation training, air-sea rescue, and communications.

RIGHT A twin-boom Blohm und Voss Bv 138 maritime reconnaissance flying boat taking off in rough seas. A total of 276 Bv 138s were operated by the Luftwaffe in Norway, France, and the Black Sea.

THE TIDE BEGINS TO TURN

In the meantime, the Catalina was playing a dominant role in the Pacific war. Following the fall of Hong Kong, Singapore, and the Dutch East Indies, RAF flying boats of 205 Squadron shadowed a Japanese carrier task force preparing to launch strikes against Ceylon (Sri Lanka) at the beginning of April 1942. At the same time, the Japanese Naval High Command was planning to return to Pearl Harbor in a daring operation involving its latest reconnaissance flying boat. The new and extremely advanced long-range four-engine Kawanishi H8K2 with a range of over 4,000 miles was selected for Operation K—a flight from the Marshall Islands to Hawaii and back—a distance of some 5,500

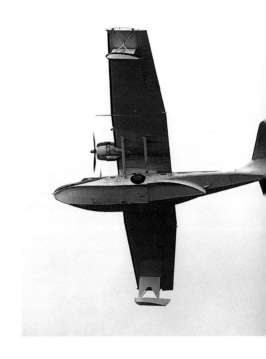

RIGHT The Royal Australian Air Force took delivery of the first of 168 Catalinas in February 1941. These included both the pure flying boat and amphibious variants, as seen here.

BELOW LEFT A US Navy "Black Cat" of VPB-34 seen at Lake Boga in Australia passing an RAAF Mariner in the background, after a three-month deployment to Manus Island in August 1944.

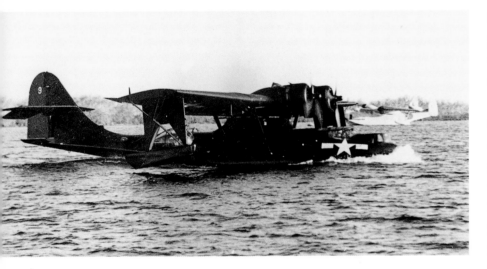

miles! The plan was to position a submarine to refuel the flying boats in a secluded atoll at the French Frigate Island between the Marshall Islands and Hawaii. On March 3, two H8K2 flying boats, codenamed "Emily" by the Allies, completed the round trip without incident but the operation failed due to bad weather obscuring the target, Pearl Harbor. Three days later, one of the "Emily" flying boats attempted a reconnaissance flight over Midway Island but was shot down by US fighters. Thus the Japanese Navy was deprived of any intelligence from Pearl Harbor or Midway Island prior to Operation Midway scheduled for early June 1942. It was a flying boat, a US Navy PBY-5, that first

sighted the Japanese Midway Task Force on June 3. This was the prelude to the Battle of Midway which effectively turned the tide of the Pacific War when the Japanese Navy suffered its first clear-cut defeat of the war.

By early 1943, 11 and 20 (RAAF) Squadron Catalinas had taken part in Operation Watchtower, attacking Japanese shipping off Rabaul, laying mines, and dropping supplies to Allied troops gaining a foothold on the Solomon Islands, losing two 'boats in the process. Later in the year US-developed airborne radar was being used by US Navy Fleet Air Wing 7 and 43 (RAAF) Squadron Catalinas, enabling them to attack Japanese shipping in New Guinea waters at night. Painted matt black, these nocturnal hunters were known as "Black Cats."

HUNTING U-BOATS

Allied flying boats were now deployed to every theater of the war, operating from Canada, the USA, Brazil, Great Britain, Gibraltar, Malta, West Africa, Madagascar, Ceylon, Australasia, and the Pacific Islands.

However, 1943 saw the resurgence of the German U-boat menace. Large packs of new long-range U-boats fitted with up to four 30mm cannon wreaked havoc with slow convoys and came close to winning the Battle of the Atlantic. Following the loss of a number of Coastal Command Sunderlands shot down by the

LEFT A dramatic shot of the crew of this battered 230 Squadron Sunderland I scrambling ashore near Derna in Libya after being shot down by an enemy aircraft during Operation *Crusader* to relieve Tobruk in December 1941.

BELOW Few Martin PBM-3 Mariners were seen in Europe, although almost 1,300 were built. They served as US Navy sub-hunters in North and South America and the Pacific, and as transports with the RAAF as seen here.

U-boats, four additional forward firing .303in guns were fitted into the nose of the latest Mark III boats, bringing the total to 12, which prompted the Germans to give it the nickname "Stachelschwein" meaning "Porcupine."

Several Luftwaffe fighters found the "Porcupine" a formidable foe, as was illustrated in June 1943 when a 461 Squadron Sunderland was attacked over the Bay of Biscay by eight Ju 88s of KG-40. The battle lasted almost an hour, during which time three German fighters were shot down and another damaged. The battered flying boat, with one of its crew killed, managed to limp home on three engines to make a forced landing on a beach in Cornwall. A few days earlier, another of 461 Squadron's boats had damaged its hull in a rough-sea landing to pick up 16 crew from a ditched bomber and the crew of another Sunderland that had sunk attempting to rescue them. With the Sunderland's hull holed during a hazardous take-off, the pilot was later able to land safely on a grass airfield in South Wales.

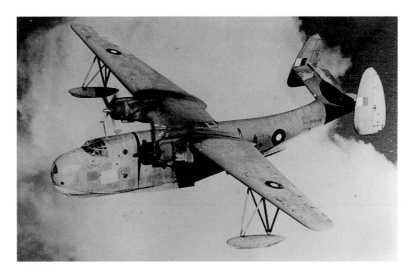

RIGHT Known by a variety of names in the Royal Navy, including the "Shagbat," Steam Pigeon, and the Flying Gas Ring, some 740 Walruses were built alongside Supermarine's Spitfire fighter at Southampton.

Meanwhile, on the other side of the Atlantic, a US Navy PBM-3 Mariner managed to pick up 48 survivors cast adrift in high seas from the merchantman *Cape San Juan* sunk by a U-boat, while the US Navy Catalina unit VP-63 began operations from Pembroke Dock in Wales, alongside RAF Coastal Command Sunderland squadrons in July 1943.

That month, the Royal Navy despatched a task force toward the Norwegian coast as part of Operation *Governor*, an Allied deception plan to mislead the Germans into thinking that southern Norway was about to be invaded. Five Luftwaffe Bv 138 flying boats of KFG 406 were catapult-launched during the night of July 26 from the seaplane tender *Buzzard* based in Trondheim Fjord to shadow the fleet. Over the next few hours four of the German boats were shot down by Martlett fighters from the carrier HMS *Illustrious*, which was part of the task force, and by marauding Beaufighters from the Shetlands. Three crew from one of the downed Bv 138s were picked up by a U-boat. However,

three days later U-489 was damaged by an RAF Hudson which forced it to stay on the surface off northwest Scotland. The following day it was spotted and attacked by two 423 Squadron Sunderlands from Lough Erne, Northern Ireland, one of which was hit by the U-boat's quadruple 20mm cannon and crashed into the sea nearby. Minutes later, Royal Navy warships were on the scene to rescue not only the stricken U-boat's crew of 54 and the three German aircrew, but also six survivors from the downed Sunderland.

ABOVE LEFT A Boeing-built PB2B-2R Catalina IVB of one of the RAAF's four "Black Cat" squadrons, 43 Squadron, used for night attacks and minelaying during 1945, with radar fairing above the cockpit and floats retracted.

BELOW The QANTAS Catalina *Spica Star* boarding passengers at the Swan River terminal at Perth for another 3,500-mile "Double Sunrise" flight to Koggala in Ceylon on the "Horseshoe Route."

BELOW LEFT From June 1943 to VE-Day, RAF Transport Command and BOAC used "semi-civilized" Sunderland III flying boats on the West Africa, Karachi, and later Calcutta routes from Poole in England to connect with QANTAS Catalinas.

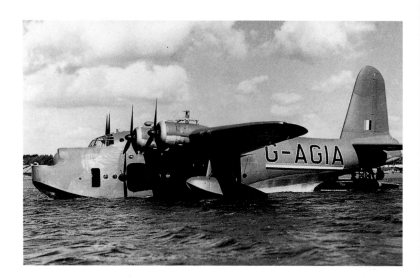

RIGHT A total of 3,290 Catalina flying boats of all types, including the amphibious variants, were produced by five different companies in the USA, Canada, and the Soviet Union between 1935 and 1945.

BELOW A Royal New Zealand Air Force 6 Sqn PBY-5 Catalina is manhandled to its mooring in the Segond Channel in the New Hebrides by its groundcrew in 1944.

BOMBING RAIDS AND RESCUE MISSIONS

By the end of 1943, the Allies had virtual control of the Mediterranean following victories in North Africa and Sicily and the surrender of Italy, while US and Australian forces were making considerable gains in the Pacific. On January 30, 1944 US Navy flying boats made one of the longest bombing raids of the campaign when two squadrons of four-engine Consolidated PB2Y-3 Coronadoes, a type which was mainly used as long-range

transports or US Admirals' barges, flew a 2,000-mile round trip from Midway Island to carry out a night attack on Japanese positions on Wake Island, both stepping stones on Pan Am's pre-war Pacific Clipper routes.

One of the busiest RAF flying boat bases outside of Great Britain was Koggala in Ceylon where Catalinas of 205, 240, and 413 Squadrons, and Sunderlands of 230 and 240 Squadrons were based. In February and March 1944 two 230 Squadron Sunderland IIIs were deployed to Assam to fly from the Monsoon-swollen Brahmaputra River to Lake Indawgyi in Burma to evacuate 537 wounded Chindits of General Wingate's Long Range Penetration Group. Koggala was also used as one end of BOAC's broken "Horseshoe Route." QANTAS used semi-civilized Catalinas on a weekly non-stop service from Swan River near Perth to Koggala. The 3,518-mile route took an average of 32 hours in the air, most of which had to be flown in radio silence, and 271 trans-ocean flights were completed without incident between November 1943 and July 1945.

Although slower, smaller, and less well-armed than the Sunderland, the Catalina's reliability, endurance, and seaworthiness made it extremely popular with its crews. However, their

confidence in the flying boat sometimes had tragic consequences. Flt Lt D E Hornell of 162 (RCAF) Squadron was awarded a posthumous VC (Victoria Cross) for an exceptionally courageous attack on a U-boat during which his Canadian Vickers-built Catalina was shot down, killing all of the seven-man crew. On July 17, 1944 Flight Officer John Cruikshank attacked U-347 in his 210 Squadron Catalina IV 700 miles north of its base at Sullom Voe in the Shetlands. The 'boat was hit 72 times and Cruikshank was severely wounded by the U-boat's 20mm cannon before the submarine was sunk by the Catalina's 500lb bombs. Despite his injuries, the pilot managed to fly back to his base and land safely. Fg Off Cruikshank was awarded the VC. More typical was another courageous attack that did not make the headlines at the time. On August 26 the pilot of a 265 Squadron Catalina IB based at Diego Suarez in Madagascar, Fg Off "Jock" Lough, pressed home a determined attack on U-862 in the Mozambique

Channel when the submarine's gunners opened up with 20mm and 37mm cannon. The Catalina was hit in the fuel tanks and the burning flying boat crashed into the sea 50 yards from the U-boat, killing the crew of nine.

Apart from hunting U-boats, the Catalina was also involved in numerous dramatic air-sea rescues. On October 24, 1944 Russian-born "Black Cat" pilot, Fg Off Armand Etienne flew 900 miles into enemy territory to rescue the crew of a 42 (RAAF) Squadron Catalina forced down on the sea off Macassar while five VPB-34 "Black Cats" rescued survivors of a US destroyer torpedoed in Ormoc Bay, western Leyte, one of which picked up 63 sailors in a single operation on December 4. However, by the

TOP Dornier's Do-24 was originally designed for the Netherlands Naval Air Service but served in the maritime reconnaissance, air-sea rescue, and transport roles with the Luftwaffe in World War Two.

LEFT US Navy PBY-5As at Naval Air Station Pensacola in Florida, the first amphibious version of the Consolidated Model 28 which was also built by Canadian Vickers from 1943 and was known as the Canso.

RIGHT Three Air France LeO H-246 26-passenger flying boats were seized by the Luftwaffe in 1942 and used by KG 200 for clandestine flights in support of German secret agents throughout Western Europe and North Africa.

RIGHT A rare shot of the prototype Blohm und Voss Bv 238 in flight. The sole example of the six-engine flying boat, which had a wingspan of almost 200 feet, was destroyed on Lake Schaal by USAAF P-51s in 1945.

end of the year the Battle of the Atlantic had turned in favor of the Allies and the U-boat packs were on the defensive. Although land-based very long-range (VLR) Liberators were proving to be Coastal Command's most effective U-boat killer, a new version of the Sunderland powered by the same engines as the Liberator and the Catalina, 1,200hp Pratt & Whitney Twin Wasps, entered service with 228 Squadron in February, 1945. Another new flying boat to make its maiden flight during this period was the Blohm und Voss Bv 238, which, with a wingspan of 197 feet 4 inches, was the largest flying boat to fly during World War Two, but the prototype was destroyed on Lake Schaal by USAAF Mustangs and further development was abandoned.

THE WAR ENDS

In the meantime, its smaller brother, the Bv 222 had been used for numerous transport flights to North Africa (during which two of the giant flying boats were shot down by RAF fighters), and for U-boat support missions over the North Atlantic (when one shot down an RAF Lancaster bomber). The type was also used by a clandestine Luftwaffe unit, KG 200, which was designed to support German secret agents throughout the continents of Europe and Africa. This undercover group also operated three former Air France four-engine LeO H-246 flying boats, one of which was shot down by RAF Hurricanes over the Mediterranean.

With the Allied noose closing around Japan, naval Kawanishi "Emilies" were being used for a number of desperate missions. On March 11, two 801st Naval Air Corps flying boats took part in Operation *Tan*, leading 24 kamikaze bombers in a 1,500-mile flight to suicide attacks on a US Naval Task Force at the Ulithi Atoll in the Caroline Islands. In the event, the Japanese formation was delayed by bad weather and only 11 kamikaze aircraft reached the target, which was then in darkness. The carrier USS *Randolph* was the only warship damaged in the raid while the H8K2s returned safely to their base on Kyushu, Japan. A week later, a transport version of the "Emily" en route from Ambon in Java to Japan was attacked by a US Navy PB4Y-1 Liberator which had to break off the engagement when it ran short of fuel. On board the badly damaged flying boat were 33 passengers and crew, one of whom was Vice Admiral Seigo Yamagata. After making a forced landing on the mudflats of a river estuary on the China coast, the "Emily" was overrun by Chinese troops and Admiral Yamagata commited hara-kiri to avoid capture. In the weeks that followed, some twenty-five H8K2 flying boats were destroyed at their moorings by "Black Cats" as the Allies mopped up resistance in Pacific islands still held by the Japanese.

In Europe, the Allies were also on the brink of victory with Soviet forces advancing along the Baltic Coast as far as the River Oder in March, supported by single-engine Soviet Naval Beriev MBR-2 flying boats. Following Hitler's suicide on April 30, a Luftwaffe Bv 138 flying boat was ordered to fly from its base in

ABOVE A diesel-engined Blohm und Voss Bw 222, one of 13 giant Viking flying boats built for the Luftwaffe as long-range maritime reconnaissance and transport aircraft, four of which were shot down.

OPPOSITE RIGHT A 210 Squadron Sunderland V in the RAF Museum, Hendon which was delivered in February 1945. Clearly shown are the retractable front gun turret and the four fixed forward-firing .303in guns in the nose.

BELOW Twin Wasp-engine RAF Sunderland Vs of the Norwegian 330 Squadron which covered the northern Atlantic in 1945 from Sullom Voe in the Shetland Islands.

Copenhagan to Lake Havel in Berlin to pick up two important government couriers. However, contact could not be made so the pilot, lieutenant-colonel Klemusch flew 10 wounded soldiers out of Berlin under heavy Soviet shellfire.

On May 3–4, RAF Typhoon and Tempest fighter-bombers and Coastal Command aircraft carried out devastating attacks on German shipping in the Baltic prior to the Allied liberation of Norway. Many of the Luftwaffe's surviving Norwegian-based flying boats including five Bv 138s, more than a dozen Do 24s, and a single Bv 222 Viking taking part in the planned German evacuation from Norway, were destroyed. The last U-boat to be sunk in the Battle of the Atlantic, and the 196th destroyed by Coastal Command aircraft, was sent to the bottom by an RAF

Catalina IV of 210 Squadron on May 7, one day before Germany's unconditional surrender.

The RAF's last official wartime patrol was flown by a 201 Squadron Sunderland III on June 3 which took off from Lough Erne in Northern Ireland for a convoy escort and anti-submarine sortie—there were still some U-boats in the Atlantic that were not accounted for. However, the Luftwaffe's last official operational mission did not take place for another two weeks when 15 Do 24 flying boats of SNG 81 flew 450 wounded German POWs from their base at Guldborg in Denmark to Schleswig, in Germany, escorted by RAF Typhoons. When the mission was completed on June 18, the Luftwaffe flying boat crews officially surrendered and marched into captivity.

CHAPTER 6

During nearly six years of World War Two, more than 9,000 multi-engine flying boats were produced by all the main protagonists, fulfilling numerous roles including maritime reconnaissance bombing, air-sea rescue, fleet spotting, long-range transport, and communications.

LEFT One of the most advanced flying boats ever to fly was the four-jet powered Martin P6M-1 SeaMaster designed for the US Navy for mine-laying, reconnaissance, air-refueling, and nuclear bombing.

ABOVE The world's first turboprop-powered flying boat, the Convair R3Y-1 Tradewind was capable of refueling from US Navy submarines at sea.

MARTIN P6M-2 SEAMASTER

Jet-powered long-range reconnaissance flying boat with a crew of five was ordered by the **US Navy** for mine-laying and maritime reconnaissance but canceled in 1959 due to high cost.

STATISTICS

Wingspan	100ft	
Length	134ft	
Height	31ft	
Weight	Empty 110,000lb	Loaded 150,000lb
Engines	Four 17,200lb st Pratt & Whitney J75 turbojets	
Max speed	630mph	
Cruise speed	600mph	
Range	3,000 miles	
Armament	2 x 20mm cannon in remote tail turret 30,000lb bombload	

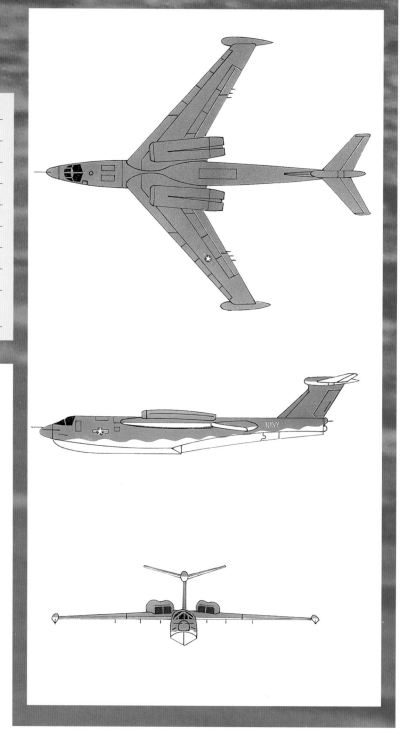

At the end of the war, more than 1,000 flying boats and amphibians remained in service with the US Navy and Army Air Force, while some 250 Sunderlands remained in service with the RAF, RAAF, (Royal New Zealand Air Force) RNZAF, and French Navy. However, time was running out, and a little over a decade later the military flying boat would appear to be a dying breed on the verge of extinction.

DECLINE SETS IN

With the termination of hostilities in 1945 came the cancellation of contracts for many advanced and innovative flying boat designs. In the United States, orders for 20 long-range transport versions of the giant Martin Mars, originally designed as a maritime reconnaissance bomber, were reduced to only five aircraft. In addition, the future of the largest flying boat in the world, the Hughes HK-1 air transporter, was even more doubtful.

An $18 million contract awarded to the Kaiser-Hughes
Corporation in 1944 for three of these massive wooden flying
boats was cut back to one at the end of the war, and another
$7 million of Howard Hughes' own money had to be spent
getting the Hughes H-4 "Spruce Goose" completed in 1946.
Almost a year later on November 2, 1947 Howard Hughes made a
one-mile flight in the 320-foot wingspan eight-engine boat at
Long Beach, California, after which it was stored under armed
guard in a controlled air-conditioned hangar for 30 years before
being donated to an aircraft museum.

There was a similar situation in Great Britain with production
orders for the Short Seaford, designed to replace the RAF
Sunderland, cut from 30 to six which were then converted to civil
transports for BOAC. Conceived as a long-range reconnaissance

LEFT A contemporary
Saunders-Roe advertisement for the
RAF Coastal Command version of
the Princess flying boat which could
carry 200 troops.

ABOVE The Hughes H-4 "Spruce
Goose," the largest flying boat ever
built, preparing for its delayed first
flight at Long Beach, California in
November 1947.

TOP An RAF Coastal Command
Sunderland V of 230 Squadron
operating from Gibraltar during
Exercise *Longreach*, a combined
Home and Mediterranean Fleet
exercise in 1946.

An even more radical British flying boat design appeared alongside the Seagull at the 1947 Society of British Aircraft Companies (SBAC) show at Farnborough: the Saunders-Roe SR A1. Developed during the war by the Empire Boat designer Sir Arthur Gouge, the SR A1 was a single-seat jet fighter flying boat. Powered by two 3.850lb thrust Metro-Vickers Beryl turbojets and armed with four 20mm Hispano cannon, the fighter flying boat, one of the first of its type since the Hansa-Brandenburgs of World War One, could also carry two 1,000lb bombs or eight rockets and was the first fighter aircraft to be fitted with a Martin-Baker

flying boat, the Short Shetland was the largest flying boat to be built in Britain when it flew at the end of 1944. Powered by four 2,500hp Bristol Centaurus engines, the 150-foot wingspan boat was not ordered by the RAF and a second prototype, which flew in 1947, was completed as a 40-passenger civil transport.

The Seagull ASR1, which flew on July 18, 1948, was the last of the Supermarine flying boats. It was designed to replace the Fleet Air Arm's Walrus and Sea Otter air-sea rescue (ASR) amphibians. Powered by 1,815hp Rolls-Royce Griffon engines, the Seagull gained the world air speed record for amphibians at a speed of 241.9mph in July, 1950. However, none were ordered, as helicopters had taken over the ASR role by the early 1950s.

TOP The Fleet Air Arm's last biplane, Supermarine's Sea Otter air-sea rescue amphibian was the last of a long line that stretched back to R J Mitchell's Seagull, and remained in production until 1946.

RIGHT The first prototype twin-jet SR A1 flying boat fighter, seen here on its beaching gear, was armed with two 20mm cannon and fitted with the first Martin-Baker ejector seat.

ABOVE RIGHT One of 10 Sealand IL amphibians, Short's last flying boat design, purchased by the Indian Navy in 1953 and served with its Fleet Requirements Unit for 10 years.

ejector seat. Three prototypes were ordered, with the first flying on July 16, 1947. Unfortunately, the second and third SR A1s crashed into the sea during flight trials by which time its performance had been outpaced by land-based fighters and the project was abandoned in 1951. Ironically, when the SR A1 appeared at the 1948 Farnborough Air Show no less than three other new flying boats took part in the flying programme: the Supermarine Seagull, the Short Solent, and the Short Sealand amphibian, small numbers of which were later operated by the Yugoslav and Indian navies.

Despite the failure of many new flying boat projects, wartime veterans were flying as intensively as ever. In the months following VE Day, RAF Sunderlands were busy flying POWs home from German ports while RAAF Catalinas were flying long-distance missions, each carrying 20 former Japanese POWs from Malaya and the Philippines to Australia after VJ Day. However, within a very short time the Cold War had broken out in Europe and RAF flying boats found themselves part of a lifeline to their former enemy.

Following a Soviet blockade of Allied-occupied Berlin in June 1948, the United States and Great Britain began flying supplies into the beleaguered city. On July 4, Sunderlands from 201 and 230 Squadrons flew into Lake Havel in the center of Berlin.

Stripped of their anti-submarine equipment, the flying boats were loaded with 10,000lbs of supplies at the old Blohm und Voss works on the River Elbe near Hamburg. Up to three six-and-a-half hour sorties a day were flown to Berlin; with no approach aids at either end and the possibility of being "buzzed" by Soviet fighters en route, all flying was carried out under visual flight rules at a height of 1,000 feet. The Sunderlands carried salt, which only the flying boats could carry, meat, and later, because of the excellent security of loading the aircraft from barges, cigarettes, and banknotes. On return flights they carried industrial goods and sick children. When ice on Lake Havel brought the Sunderland airlift to a halt six months later, the flying boats had carried nearly 5,000 tons of freight into Berlin during Operation *Plainfare* and had brought out more than 1,000 refugees.

ABOVE Two Grumman Mallard amphibians, delivered to the Royal Egyptian Air Force in 1949 and used by King Farouk's Royal Flight before he was forced to abdicate in 1952.

LEFT The world's first jet fighter flying boat, the Saunders-Roe SR A1, seen taking off from the Solent in England in July 1947 with test pilot Geoffrey Tyson at the controls.

THE KOREAN WAR

As the Berlin Airlift was winding down, a larger and potentially more dangerous conflict was about to break out on the other side of the world. An RAF Sunderland had already been involved in a confrontation with Communist forces at the height of the civil war in China. On April 21, 1949, an 88 Squadron Sunderland was fired on by the Communist Chinese after landing alongside the Royal Navy frigate HMS *Amethyst* which had gone aground in the Yangtze River. Although it suffered a number of hits, the Sunderland, which had been carrying a doctor and medical supplies, was able to take off successfully and for the next two days it returned to the stricken warship and was again damaged by ground fire. A year later North Korea, aided by Communist China, invaded South Korea and the United Nations became involved in its first war.

Within mere days of the outbreak of the Korean War, RAF Sunderlands of 88 Squadron were again in action and in February 1951 205 Squadron's flying boats were giving air cover to UN naval forces bombarding North Korean coastal towns. The aircraft of the Seletar Sunderland Wing made up of 88, 205, and 209 Squadrons were based at Iwakuni in southern Japan on four-week detachments from Malaya, 3,000 miles away. They carried out round-the-clock searches for enemy shipping and submarines in the Tsushima Straits as part of the UN blockade of the north. The Sunderlands, the only RAF aircraft to give operational service throughout the entire conflict, flew a total of 1,647 sorties.

The British 'boats were joined by USAF OA-10B and US Navy PB4Y-2 Catalinas based in Japan, and PBM-5 Mariners of VP-6, VP-42, and VP-47. The latter were attached to Task Group 99.2 from Iwakuni during the Battle of Inchon and in October 1950 the Mariners, joined by RAF Sunderlands, were requested to support a US Marine Corps attack on Wonsan by firing their guns into unmarked minefields, but this proved to be an unsatisfactory method of clearing mines. On July 31, 1951 a Mariner of VP-6 was attacked by two MiG-15s which killed two of the crew and wounded two more. The US Navy's four operational Martin JRM-1 Mars flying boats of VR-2 were heavily involved in the war, flying freight or up to 132 troops or 84 stretcher patients plus 25 medical attendants between their base at Naval Air Station (NAS) Alameda, California and Honolulu. During this period one of VP-2's big logistic 'boats carried a total of 301 sailors plus a crew of seven on a flight from San Francisco to San Diego.

The USAF's new twin-engine Grumman SA-16A Albatross amphibian was rushed into overseas service with the 3rd Air Rescue Squadron (ARS) at Taegu in July 1950, replacing OV-10B Cats. Maintaining continuous daylight search and rescue (SAR) patrols over the Tsushima Straits, the SA-16s were subsequently responsible for the rescue of some 100 downed airmen during the four-year conflict, many from behind enemy lines and under fire from enemy forces. A typical mission took place in June 1951

ABOVE The US Navy deployed three squadrons of World War Two vintage Martin PBM-5 Mariners to Iwakuni in Japan during the early months of the Korean War, one of which is seen here in 1949.

TOP RIGHT A number of Japan-based US Navy Catalinas, such as this PB2B-2 "Black Cat" amphibian at Itazuke in 1951, supported United Nations forces fighting in Korea.

when Lt J Najarian put down his Albatross on the Taedong River under intense fire at night to snatch a downed F-51 Mustang pilot to safety. A year later, another SA-16 rescued Maj Frederick Blesse, at the time the USAF's leading Sabre "ace," after he had been shot down over the Yellow Sea.

THE COLD WAR

The period was one of increasing political tension worldwide and flying boats continued to play their part, often with tragic results. In Europe, the Cold War was hotting up. On June 18, 1952, Soviet MiG-17s shot down a Swedish Air Force C-47 Dakota over international waters of the Baltic killing 10 crew. Two Swedish Air Force Catalinas were involved in a search for the missing aircraft, one of which was itself attacked by MiGs later the same day, forcing it to land on the Baltic near Hummand Island. Two of the crew were injured.

Soon after the end of the Korean War, USAF SA-16As and an RAF Sunderland were involved in another shoot-down. On July 23, 1954 a Cathay Pacific DC4 carrying 12 passengers and six crew en route from Bangkok to Hong Kong, was shot down without warning by two Communist Chinese La-9 fighters outside Chinese airspace near Hainan Island. Nine of the passengers and crew were killed in the attack but the rest managed to get into a life-raft before the stricken airliner sank. They had been able to send out an SOS which was picked up at Clark Field in Manila and two Albatrosses of the 31st Air Rescue Squadron (ARS) were launched to search an area nearly 700 miles away.

Meanwhile, an 88 Squadron Sunderland from Hong Kong was on the scene but the life-raft had drifted into a small bay at Timboas Island and the flying boat was unable to land due to high waves and a restricted landing run. At the same time, the

Chinese were threatening to shoot down any military aircraft in the area, but Capt Jack Woodyard in one of the 31st ARS SA-16s was already over the survivors and managed to put his Albatross down in the heavy swell using his reversible propellers to bring it to a halt while a French Privateer circled overhead to give warning of any attack and to guide him to the life-raft. It took the amphibian almost an hour to taxi two miles across the heavy seas. After taking on board the survivors, one of whom died within minutes of being rescued, the SA-16A managed to take off using jet-assisted take off (JATO) and flew them to Hong Kong to complete the journey they had begun nearly 24 hours earlier.

NEW DEVELOPMENTS AND FALSE STARTS

In the meantime, the Korean War had sparked renewed interest in the flying boat, particularly in the United States where several new advanced designs appeared in the mid-1950s. One of the most successful of these was Glenn L Martin's replacement for the Mariner, the P5M-1 Marlin. Powered by two 3,250hp Wright R-3350 Turbo Compound piston engines, the Marlin had a wingspan of 118 feet, carried a crew of eight, and had a maximum speed of 250mph with a range of over 2,000 miles. Its equipment included an AN/APS-44 search radar, twin 20mm cannon in a remote-

RIGHT A US Navy Martin P5M-1 Marlin anti-submarine warfare flying boat of VP-44 docking in a rubber U-dock alongside the LST USS *Ashland* in 1957.

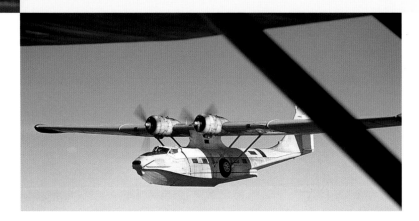

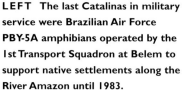

LEFT The last Catalinas in military service were Brazilian Air Force PBY-5A amphibians operated by the 1st Transport Squadron at Belem to support native settlements along the River Amazon until 1983.

CENTER LEFT The first prototype of Convair's advanced jet fighter flying boat, the XF2Y-1, taxies out into San Diego Bay under its own power in December 1952.

BOTTOM LEFT The delta-wing single-seat Convair XF2Y-1, the fastest flying boat ever built, on its unique single V-shaped hydro-ski during a high speed take-off run across San Diego Bay during sea trials in 1953.

controlled radar-operated rear turret, and a unique Martin-designed "Hydroflap" fitted to each side of the rear hull which opened to 65 degrees to act as a landing brake and turning aid on the water. The P5M-1 made its first flight in June 1951 and the first Marlins were delivered to VP-40 at San Diego, California in April 1952, but the US Navy's new anti-submarine warfare (ASW) flying boat came too late to prove itself during the Korean War. Seven P4M-1s, out of 121 produced between 1951 and 1954 were operated by the US Coast Guard.

The most exciting of the new generation flying boats was the Convair Sea Dart, a supersonic jet fighter flying boat. Having watched the development of the British SR A1 with interest, the US Navy embarked on the Sea Dart programme pushing state-of-the-art aerodynamics and hydrodynamics to the limit.

A slim thin-winged delta single-seater powered by two 4,080lb thrust afterburning Westinghouse XJ46 turbojets, the Sea Dart was designed to take off and land on retractable hydro-skis! The pressurized cockpit near the end of the pointed nose was equipped with an ejector seat. The first of five Sea Darts flew in great secrecy at San Diego on April 9, 1953 and, although the aircraft suffered from poor stability and lack of power on take-off,

flight trials continued without mishap for two-and-a-half years during which time it became the first, and only, flying boat to break the sound barrier when the YF2Y-1 Sea Dart exceeded Mach 1 in a shallow dive on August 3, 1954. However, three months later the same aircraft disintegrated during a high-speed run at 500 feet on its first public demonstration at San Diego. Test pilot Charles E Richbourg was killed and the viability of high-speed fighter flying boats was thrown into some doubt. Although successful open sea landings had previously been made, the Sea Dart required near perfect sea conditions in which to operate and "ski-porpoising" problems persisted until the project was eventually canceled in 1956.

Convair, which produced the Catalina, had also developed a very different flying boat at the same time as the Sea Dart, the first turboprop-powered four-engine long-range transport flying boat—the Tradewind. Derived from the XP5Y-1, a prototype

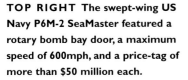

TOP RIGHT The swept-wing US Navy P6M-2 SeaMaster featured a rotary bomb bay door, a maximum speed of 600mph, and a price-tag of more than $50 million each.

ABOVE AND BELOW The US Navy's R3Y-2 "Flying LST" version of the world's first turboprop-powered flying boat, the Convair Tradewind, with a hinged nose section, seen refueling four Grumman F9F-8 Cougar fighters.

reconnaissance bomber which flew for the first time at San Diego on April 18, 1950, two versions of the large graceful Tradewind were produced in small numbers for the US Navy. Both had a 145-foot wingspan and were powered by four 5,850shp Allison T40 turboprops. The fully pressurized R3Y-1 was 142 feet long and could accommodate a crew of seven, plus 103 troops or 92 stretcher patients and 12 medical attendants, while the 139-foot long R3Y-2 was designed as a "Flying LST" (Landing Ship Tank) to taxi up to a beachhead and disembark 155mm Howitzers, jeeps, or assault troops using built-in ramps under the nose that hinged it upward. Both variants could be used to air-refuel up to four US Navy fighters. A total of 11 Tradewinds, with a maximum speed of nearly 400mph and a range of 4,500 miles at 300mph, were operated by the US Navy's Fleet Logistic Wing alongside the Martin JRM-1/2 Mars from 1954, but due to the unreliability of the early Allison turboprops they were withdrawn from service in 1958.

Perhaps the most advanced flying boat ever to be produced in the United States was the Martin SeaMaster, the world's first multi-jet engine flying boat. Designed as an anti-submarine aircraft, minelayer, and nuclear bomber, the SeaMaster had four 13,000lb thrust afterburning Allison J71 turbojets mounted above the shoulder-mounted swept wing with wingtip floats and a high "T" tail to avoid spray when taking off and landing on water. The first of two prototype XP6M-1s made a successful first flight on July 14, 1955. However, within 18 months both had been lost in accidents in the air due to failures of the tailplane trimmers.

Nevertheless, the first of six pre-production P6M-1 SeaMasters flew in January 1958 and 24 production P6M-2s were ordered. These were powered by four 17,200lb thrust Pratt & Whitney J75 turbojets, giving a maximum speed of over 600mph and a range of nearly 3,000 miles. It featured the Martin "Hydroflaps," a rotary bomb bay, a remote tail turret, and a pressurized cabin for the crew of five. Special beaching vehicles and equipment for refueling from submarines at sea were developed, but by the end of 1958 orders for production P6M-2s were cut to eight aircraft. When it was discovered that these eight SeaMasters would cost almost $450 million the program was canceled a year later after three P6M-2s had flown.

An even more ambitious project was conceived by General Dynamics' Convair Division at San Diego in 1965—the GD "Sub-Plane." At the request of the US Navy, the company concluded that the development of an anti-submarine warfare flying boat submarine, with a range of 500 miles flying at 250mph powered by electric motors and batteries able to land on water and submerge with an underwater range of 50nm at 5 knots, was feasible and practical. However, the costings involved precluded any further development.

LEFT Special floating beaching vehicles were developed for advanced jet-powered Martin SeaMaster before the program was canceled in 1969.

TOP When it entered service with the US Navy in 1954, the troop-carrying version of the Tradewind, the R3Y-1, was the world's most powerful flying boat.

THE FINAL FLING

Europe in the meantime had all but abandoned military flying boat development. The Italian manufacturer Piaggio had built a small twin-engine amphibian, the P136, 23 of which were operated by the Italian Air Force for air-sea rescue and communications, while a projected twin-turboprop powered flying boat, the P166, never left the drawing board. The Korean War renewed calls for cocooned Saunders-Roe Princesses to be taken over by the RAF as a long-range transport, while the same company had proposed a four-turboprop-powered Sunderland replacement, but nothing came of it.

In fact, the Sunderland soldiered on throughout the 1950s operating from the tropics to the Arctic. In 1952–3, Sunderlands of 201 and 230 Squadrons carried 380 tons of equipment for the British Greenland Expedition from Young Sound on the northeast coast of Greenland to the expedition's base camp at Britannia Lake, 800 miles from the North Pole. During the 11-year operation conducted by British forces against Communist guerrillas in Malaya, Sunderlands flew more than 150 sorties a year from 1949 onward, while at the same time detaching flying boats to the Korean War. At the end of 1956, the veteran flying boat carried out its last air-sea rescue mission when it rescued 20 survivors from a Japanese ship off Selatar. In fact, the last RAF Sunderland sortie was flown by 205 Squadron from Selatar on May 15, 1959, when it was finally replaced by the Avro Shackleton landplane, although the type would continue to serve with the French Navy and Royal New Zealand Air Force for another decade.

TOP A US Navy P-5B Marlin leads an RNZAF Sunderland GR.5 and a RAAF P2V-7 Neptune over the South China Seas in 1963.

ABOVE Italy's only post-war multi-engine flying boat, the Piaggio P136. Some were operated by the Italian Air Force in air-sea rescue, communications, and training roles.

LEFT RAF Sunderland flying boats played an important part in the Berlin Airlift, flying more than 4,500 tons of food into Lake Havel during Operation *Plainfare* in 1948.

LEFT France produced small numbers of the Nord Noroit air-sea rescue and maritime reconnaissance amphibians for the Aéronavale during the 1950s.

BELOW A US Navy Martin SP-5B Marlin flying boat of VP-40, based at Cam Ranh Bay, flying low over a junk in the waters off South Vietnam in 1965 during Operation *Market Time*.

In the Soviet Union, the flying boat was in the ascendant. Having relied on aging Be-2s, given the NATO codename of "Mote," and Lend-Lease and license-built Catalinas known as "Mops," until the end of World War Two, the Soviet Navy ordered a new twin-engine gull-winged long-range flying boat, the Be-6 "Madge," in 1949. Developed from Beriev's LL-143, which first flew in September 1945, the Be-6 was powered by two 2,400hp ASh-73 piston engines, was heavily armed with six guns in nose, top deck, and tail turrets, and could carry a 20,000lb bombload. The 108-foot wingspan flying boat had a crew of eight, but could carry up to 40 commandos, had a maximum speed of 234mph, and a range of nearly 3,000 miles. More than 200 Be-6s were built for the Soviet forces.

In response to the Soviet Navy's requirement for a replacement for the Be-6, Beriev used its experience of flying an experimental twin-jet powered flying boat, the R-1, in 1952, to produce a large swept-wing twin-jet powered flying boat with an impressive performance that rivaled the more advanced Martin SeaMaster. The 94-foot wingspan, 100-foot long Be-10 "Mallow" maritime reconnaissance bomber carried a crew of three. Powered by two shoulder-mounted 14,330lb thrust AL-7PB turbojets, it established a number of FAI-recognized records for water-borne aircraft. These included speed (566.9mph), altitude (49,135 feet), and payload (15 tons), all set in 1961. But despite its record-breaking performance, the Be-10 was limited in range and weapons capacity and could only operate in relatively calm

waters; it was produced in small numbers and was only issued to two units of the Black Sea Fleet. Following the Cuban Missile Crisis in October 1962, Soviet Navy "Mallows" flew reconnaissance missions over Turkey to verify that US missiles had been withdrawn.

By 1965 both the Soviet Navy's Be-6 and Be-10 flying boats were in the process of being replaced by the Be-12 "Mail," a gull-winged twin-turboprop powered amphibian which was to become one of the most successful and long-lived flying boats built since World War Two. Beriev's "Tchaika" (Seagull) established more than 20 world records for turboprop amphibians in the 1960s, during which time almost 200 were delivered to the Soviet Navy's Baltic, Black Sea, and Northern Fleets and would remain in service for more than 30 years.

By the end of 1960, the last of 117 upgraded Marlins, the P-5Bs had been delivered, at the time the world's most powerfully equipped anti-submarine patrol aircraft. Ten were supplied to the French Navy, which operated several flying boats including Catalinas, Gooses, and Sunderlands, to be operated by Flottille 27F at Dakar in West Africa. The ASW equipment of US Navy

Marlins, which equipped a dozen Navy Patrol Squadrons, was continuously updated during the 1960s and they were deployed to many trouble spots around the world including Cuba, Formosa (Taiwan), and Vietnam. From May 1965, the re-designated SP-5Bs belonging to VP-40 operated from the US Navy's last operational flying boat tender, the USS *Salisbury Sound* anchored in Cam Ranh Bay off the coast of South Vietnam some 300 miles south of the Demilitarized Zone. They patrolled the Gulf of Tonkin during Operation *Market Time* searching for Communist cargo junks

ABOVE The Soviet Union's first post-war flying boat was the twin-engine, gull-wing anti-submarine and air-sea rescue flying boat, the Be-6 which was given the **NATO** codename of "Madge."

TOP The Beriev Be-10 "Mallow" jet flying boat had a crew of three with the pilot in a fighter-style cockpit, and was operated mainly in a reconnaissance role with Black Sea Fleet units.

ABOVE A contemporary of the US SeaMaster, the swept-wing twin-jet Be-10 maritime reconnaissance bomber flying boat was operated by the Soviet Navy in the early 1960s.

smuggling arms to the Vietcong, as well as Soviet and Chinese submarines operating in the area. The last patrol by an SP-5B over South Vietnamese waters took place on April 11, 1967, after which the last of the US Navy's big 'boats were flown to Japan and broken up for scrap.

The distinction of being the US Navy's last flying boat fell to the HU-16B Albatross, which was retired in 1976. More than 460 Albatrosses had been built between 1949 and 1961 for the US Air Force, Navy, and Coast Guard, and the versatile amphibian would serve with a total of 20 overseas air arms over the next three decades. As with the Marlin, its operational swansong was the Vietnam conflict. In June 1964 USAF HU-16Bs of the 31st ARS arrived at Da Nang in South Vietnam, while others were stationed at Korat in Thailand. For the next 18 months the amphibians maintained constant ASR patrols over the Gulf of Tonkin, during which time they were credited with some 50 rescues of downed US aircrew, but four amphibians were lost in action before they were replaced by Lockheed HC-130s and air-refuellable HH-3 "Jolly Green Giant" helicopters in 1967. A year previously, a Chinese Nationalist Air Force HU-16B had been shot down by Communist Chinese MiG-17s after picking up three Chinese defectors from Matsu Island.

The last US Coast Guard HU-16E was not withdrawn from service until March 1983, while overseas Albatross military operations would continue well into the 1990s, its longevity only rivaled by that of the Russian Be-12 Seagull.

RIGHT More than 200 Be-12 "Tchaika" amphibians were delivered to the Soviet Navy, some of which were operated in "friendly" nation's markings including Vietnam and, as seen here, the United Arab Republic.

OPPOSITE The last US Coast Guard Albatross amphibian, and the service's last flying boat, finally retired in March 1983 after a service life of more than 32 years.

CENTER LEFT Ten Martin P5M-2 Marlin flying boats were operated by the Aéronavale based with Flottille 27F at Dakar in West Africa from where they flew 14- to 17-hour maritime patrols in the 1960s.

ABOVE A USAF Grumman HU-16B Albatross of the 37th Air Rescue and Recovery Squadron at Kai Tak, Hong Kong, the unit that was responsible for rescuing many downed pilots during the Vietnam War.

CENTER RIGHT Both the Soviet Navy's Be-6 and Be-10 maritime reconnaissance flying boats were replaced by the versatile and sturdy amphibious Beriev Be-12 "Mail" by the end of the 1960s.

ABOVE The US Navy's last Martin SP-5B Marlin 5533, which belonged to VP-40, made its final flight at NAS North Field, San Diego in November 1967, marking the end of the US Navy's flying boat operations.

CHAPTER 7

By 1946, Pan American World Airways and BOAC had replaced the last of their flying boats on the transatlantic route with Lockheed L-049 Constellation landplanes.

LEFT Another ex-BOAC Sandringham was operated in the Pacific by the French airline RAI, which used the big 'boat to fly local services from Tahiti until 1970.

ABOVE A 1949 British West Indian Airways poster depicting a Short Sealand in the Caribbean prophetically overshadowed by a landplane.

SAUNDERS–ROE SR.45 PRINCESS

Long-range commercial flying boat with a crew of ten was built for BOAC but canceled even before the first prototype flew in 1952.

STATISTICS

Wingspan	219ft 6in	
Length	148ft	
Height	55ft 9in	
Weight	Empty 295,000lb	Loaded 345,000lb
Engines	Ten 3,200shp Bristol Proteus 600 turboprops	
Max speed	400mph	
Cruise speed	358mph	
Range	5,500 miles	
Passengers	Maximum 220	

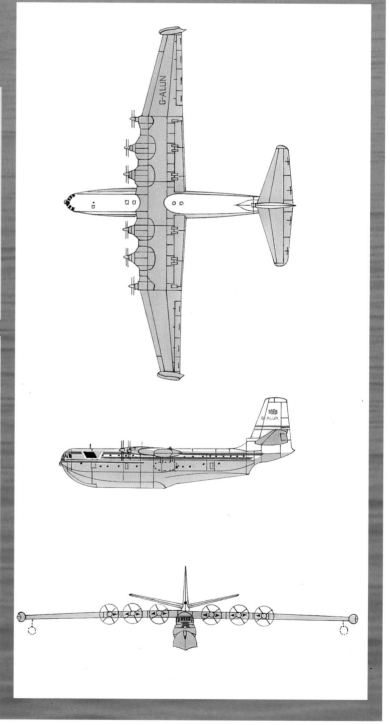

TRANSATLANTIC SWAN SONG

All of the Boeing 314s had survived the war and were sold off to some of the many new charter airlines that mushroomed at the end of the war. One of these was American International Airlines, which had acquired the former Pan Am *Capetown Clipper*, now renamed *Bermuda Sky Queen*, to operate transatlantic charter flights for oil and shipping company employees. On October 13, 1947 the flying boat took off from Poole in England en route for New York via Foynes in Ireland, and Gander, Newfoundland. The *Bermuda Sky Queen* was about to make history on two counts, the first being that it was carrying the biggest ever passenger load for a transatlantic flight—62 plus seven crew. By mid-Atlantic it became clear that, due to the fact that the Boeing was seriously overloaded and was encountering stronger than predicted headwinds, it would not have enough fuel to reach Gander. The only alternative was to land in high seas alongside the nearest US Coast Guard weather-ship, the *Bibb*. The combined skills of the

Sky Queen's pilot in bringing the flying boat down in one piece and the *Bibb*'s captain for rescuing all 69 people from the sinking aircraft averted a potential aviation disaster. However, the valiant old boat remained afloat 24 hours later and had to be sunk by fire from another USCG vessel as she was a hazard to navigation.

Other Boeing 314s, including Pan Am's *American*, *Anzac*, *California*, and *Dixie Clippers*, and the former BOAC's boats were all purchased by World Airways, which was formed in March 1948. Initially they were used for immigration charter flights between Puerto Rico and New York, but following financial problems these services were suspended in 1949. Air France re-established its transatlantic services using the six-engine 70-ton Late 631 flying boat. Designed in 1936, the war prevented the Late 631 from being completed until 1942, when it was seized by the Luftwaffe and destroyed by RAF Mosquito fighter-bombers on Lake Constance a year later. Air France had a fleet of nine of the 188-foot wingspan Late 631s that could carry 46 passengers on its North Atlantic route, which was inaugurated in August 1947. However, following the loss of one on its delivery flight and a second after a forced landing in the Atlantic, the type was withdrawn from service and the route taken over by Constellations. In 1950 three of the Late 631s were sold to France Hydro to ferry cotton to the French Cameroons, an operation that lasted until September 1955 when another boat was lost.

THE EMPIRE ROUTES

Although BOAC's last transatlantic flying boat service had been flown by a Boeing 314A in March 1946, the airline still had a sizable fleet of flying boats which it planned to use on the relaunched Empire routes. The routes to India, Singapore, and Sydney were introduced in 1946 using some of the 26 Short Hythe flying boats which were 16 to 24-passenger conversions of the Sunderland. In November 1945, Shorts had launched the first fully civilian conversion of the Sunderland, the Sandringham,

TOP BOAC Hythe *Hanwell* about to dock at the newly opened flying boat Berth 50 in Southampton Docks at the end of a scheduled flight from Karachi in 1948.

LEFT In 1947, construction of nine Late 631 transatlantic flying boats, designed for Air France in the 1930s, was completed, but after only one year flying the France–Caribbean service they were withdrawn.

LEFT The first, and the last, large commercial flying boat to be produced in Great Britain after World War Two was the Short Solent, 18 of which were ordered by BOAC in 1947 for use on its South Africa route.

RIGHT The luxurious but slow Short Sandringham with its landplane successor, the Constellation, pass each other in this 1946 BOAC poster.

which seated 22 passengers on two decks, together with a promenade deck, dining room, and cocktail bar. More spartan versions could seat up to 45 passengers and were sold to airlines in Argentina, Norway, and New Zealand, while 12 of the 26 Sandringhams built were acquired by BOAC to replace Hythes on the Far East routes in 1947. In March 1948, BOAC Plymouth Class Sandringhams enabled the Hong Kong "Dragon Route" to be extended to Iwakuni, Japan and later on to Tokyo.

The largest, the most powerful, and the last British flying boat to be operated by BOAC was the Short Solent, which entered service in March 1948. A civil version of the Short Seaford developed to replace the military Sunderland, the Solent first flew in November 1946. Powered by four 1,690hp Bristol Hercules engines, the Solent had a cruising speed of nearly 250mph and a range of 1,800 miles.

Its spacious hull enabled the standard of passenger accommodation to rival the luxury of the old Empire Boats. On the upper deck there was a large passenger cabin with lounge, a cocktail bar, the steward's compartment, and galley. On the lower deck, reached by a circular starcase, were three passenger cabins, a promenade deck, a library, dressing rooms, and toilets. Up to 39 passengers and a crew of seven were carried on BOAC flights. A total of 18 Solents were acquired by the Corporation for use on the twice-weekly "Springbok Route" flying from BOAC's new marine air terminal at Southampton, England to Johannesburg. The 6,400-mile route took four days with night stops at Augusta, Luxor, Port Bell, and Victoria Falls.

BOAC's pilots had nothing but praise for the Solent, which had an accident-free record in service. Although the type undertook route-proving flights to Australia, it was decided that the London

LEFT BOAC Solent 2 *Solway*, launched in February 1948, seen here during take-off from Southampton Water at the start of its flight to Johannesburg, South Africa.

LEFT TEAL's third Solent RMA *Awatere*, launched at Belfast in October 1949, is seen here in formation with its little brother, the only other post-war British flying boat, the Short Sealand amphibian.

BELOW Designed for BOAC, the majestic 10-engine Saunders–Roe Princess was designed to carry 105 passengers on the North Atlantic route but was canceled before it made its first flight in 1952.

BOTTOM *Aotearoa II* was sold to Aquila Airways in 1955 and is seen here at its moorings at Las Palmas a year later. Britain's last flying boat airline ceased trading in September 1958.

to Sydney route would be taken over by Constellations. By mid-1949, the Hythes and Sandringhams had been retired and were not replaced by Solents. At the beginning of 1950, BOAC announced that flying boat operations would be phased out during the next two years. However, on November 3, services abruptly ceased, with Solent G-AHIO *Somerset* leaving Southampton for the last time, bound for South Africa. Most of the three-year old Solent fleet was scrapped.

In the event, use of the marine air terminal at Southampton was continued by Aquila Airways, formed in May 1948. Using Hythes, Aquila built up a flourishing charter business flying ships' crews to Aden, Basra, and the Falkland Islands, and holidaymakers to the Scilly Isles. Having taken over some ex-BOAC Solents, the airline built up a seasonal scheduled route network that included Madeira, Las Palmas, Genoa, Capri, Montreux, and Majorca as well as trooping flights to Cyprus and, during the Suez Crisis in 1956, the evacuation of hundreds of British civilians from Fanara on Egypt's Great Bitter Lake.

In September 1956 one of Aquila's Solents was wrecked by a storm at Santa Margherita in Italy, and on November 15, 1957 Solent G-AKNU named *Sydney* crashed on the Isle of Wight. Of the 50 passengers and eight crew on the Madeira-bound flight, only 15 survived. When Aquila Solent G-ANYI *Awateri* left for Madeira on September 29, 1958 it was the last passenger-carrying flying boat to leave Southampton. The following day the airline ceased operations and closed down.

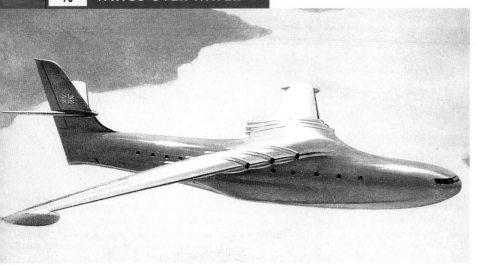

persisted in designing the even more advanced Saro Duchess, a 74-seater powered by six 5,000lb thrust de Havilland Goblin jet engines, that could travel faster and was more economical than the DH Comet, the world's first jet airliner. Unfortunately, the Duchess got no further than the drawing board, and the company withdrew from the aviation business at the end of the 1960s.

Six years earlier, the first flight of Britain's last great hope for future commercial flying boat success took place. The Saunders–Roe Princess had been built to BOAC specifications but was destined to failure from the combination of a lack of suitable engines and being politically unfashionable. Designed to carry 105 passengers between Southampton and New York, the 150-ton 'boat with a wingspan of 148 feet was powered by ten 3,200shp Bristol Proteus turboprops to give it a cruising speed of 360mph over a range of 5,250 miles.

Following BOAC's rejection of the £8 million ($22.4 million) Princess and in spite of several serious bids from Don Bennett's British South American Airways and Aquila Airways amongst others, the three completed flying boats, only one of which had flown and performed well on trials, were cocooned in 1954 "to be available to RAF Transport Command in time of emergency." When that time came two years later during the Suez Crisis, the conflict was long over before the Saro boats, each of which would be capable of carrying more than 200 troops, could be made ready, and they remained in open storage at Calshot until 1967 when they were unceremoniously scrapped.

Despite this setback, Saunders–Roe still firmly believed that there was a healthy future for commercial flying boats, and

PACIFIC ADVENTURES

While the big boats were fading into history in the United States and Europe, they continued to thrive in Australasia and the Pacific islands. Before the war, New Zealand had been on both Pan Am's and Imperial Airways' flying boat routes, and Tasman Empire Airways Ltd (TEAL) had operated two Empire Boats since 1940. In 1947, the airline acquired four Short Sandringhams to replace the veteran "C" Boats which flew their last Auckland to Sydney service on October 29, 1947. After only two years' service, the Sandringhams were sold to Australia's QANTAS and Ansett airlines and were replaced by five new upgraded Solents powered by 2,040hp Hercules engines.

TEAL's more powerful Solents could carry up to 45 passengers with a crew of seven, and from 1950 flew to Australia and Fiji, and the "Coral Route" from Auckland to Suva, the Cook Islands, and Tahiti, which was later extended to Western Samoa and Tonga. TEAL's flagship, *Aotearoa II*, which is Maori for "Land of the Long White Cloud," carried Queen Elizabeth and Prince Philip on their 1953 tour of New Zealand. Although two of the

TOP An even more advanced flying boat project from Saunders Roe was the 74-seat four-jet Saro Duchess which was designed to compete economically with contemporary jet airliners.

RIGHT Cutaway of Teal's flagship RMA *Aotearoa II*.

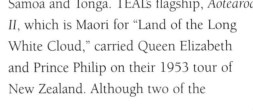

LEFT Passengers disembarking from a civilized ex-RAAF QANTAS PB2B-2 Catalina at Lord Howe Island after its flight from Sydney to Fiji in December 1947.

BELOW In 1964, the Ansett Sandringham was joined by a civilized ex-Royal New Zealand Sunderland V named *Islander* to fly the Sydney to Lord Howe Island route.

Solents were replaced on the Wellington to Sydney route by DC6s and sold to Aquila Airways in 1956, it was not until September 15, 1960 that TEAL flew its last flying boat service from Tahiti to Auckland, New Zealand.

The Sandringhams sold to QANTAS replaced civilized ex-RAAF Catalinas on the Sydney to Lord Howe Island and Fiji routes. During the war, the airline had operated the 5,000-mile Sydney to India sector of the wartime "Horseshoe Route" between Australia and England using Catalinas, and in 1947 it acquired seven more ex-RAAF PB2B-2 "Cats." They initially flew the nine-hour flight from Sydney to Noumea, New Caledonia and on for another six hours to Fiji. They soldiered on in New Guinea, flying their last service from Port Moresby to Sydney in August 1958.

Several other civilized "Cats" had colorful careers in the orient. In 1948, a Cathay Pacific Catalina flying from Hong Kong was seized by pirates and its passengers robbed of cash and valuables, while another Hong Kong ex-USAAF "Cat" registered VR-HDH made a living after the war flying gamblers and their gold from Hong Kong to casinos in nearby Portuguese Macao. In 1962 it was sold to Trans Australia Airlines and operated its "Sunbird" Services in Papua New Guinea until 1968. Ex-RAAF Catalina VH-BDP was purchased by American mercenary Ralph R Colbey, who flew the amphibian for Indonesia's General Sukarto during his struggle for independence from the Dutch in 1948, the same year that Asian Airlines, registered in Singapore, tried to set up a base at Lake Boga in Australia for its fleet of nine Catalinas. However, following a report that the Commonwealth Security Branch was investigating Asian Airlines in relation to its possible interest in Communist terrorist activities in Malaya, the project fell through and plans were subsequently aborted.

Lord Howe Island, 420 miles out into the Pacific Ocean from Sydney, had become an important tourist resort in the 1930s, one that was quickly revived for war-weary holidaymakers after 1945. QANTAS and Trans Oceanic Airways, both flying Catalinas, began flying boat services to the island in 1946. Competition was fierce and when one of QANTAS' boats exploded and sank in Sydney's Rose Bay Water Airport in August 1949, a Trans Oceanic Airways employee was accused but later acquitted. QANTAS Sandringhams were introduced on the route in 1950. Trans Oceanic purchased three ex-BOAC Solent Starliners in 1951 to operate services between Sydney and Port Moresby and to Hobart, but following the loss of *Star of Hobart* after hitting a dredger in Sydney harbor, the airline went into liquidation and its Lord Howe Island route was taken over by Ansett Airways in 1953.

Meanwhile, Trans Oceanic's founder, Capt Brian Monkton, had formed a new airline, South Pacific Airlines, using the two Solents of his former venture plus another ex-BOAC boat to operate a twice-weekly service between Honalulu and Tahiti via Christmas

Island. However, following the British government's decision to use the Christmas Island area as an atomic bomb testing range, South Pacific also went into liquidation in 1955 before operating the route, and its three Solents were sold to the eccentric billionaire and erstwhile flying boat constructor, Howard Hughes.

For the 21 years the two Ansett Sandringhams, one of which was replaced by a civilized ex-RNZAF Sunderland in 1963, operated from Rose Bay, one of the last fully equipped commercial flying boat bases in the world, flying the ever popular Lord Howe Island route. In 1974 an airstrip was built on the island and these

ABOVE The former RAF/RNZAF Sunderland *Islander* was sold by Ansett in 1975 to Antilles Air Boats in the US Virgin Islands, where it operated until 1979 when it was purchased by British millionaire Edward Hulton.

BELOW The last flying boats operated by Pan Am were Grumman Albatrosses, two of which flew between the Mariana, Caroline, and Marshall Islands in Micronesia under contract to the US Trust Territories.

two surviving big 'boats were sold to an ex-American Export Airlines pilot, Charles Blair, who had formed a flying boat-equipped airline in the US Virgin Islands.

Two other flying boat operations of note in the Pacific were those of RAI, based in French Tahiti and linking Papeete with the Society and Tuamotu Islands. In 1958, a 45-seat ex-BOAC Sandringham which had been flying charter cruises around New Guinea and the Pacific Islands for four years replaced RAI's two Catalinas. The French-registered flying boat was operated by the local Tahiti-based airline until 1970, supplementing its Grumman Mallard, 27 years after it was launched as an RAF Sunderland.

Although Pan Am had retired the last of its big 'boats in 1947, it did not fly its last flying boat operations until almost 25 years later. In July 1960, Pan Am won a contract from the US Trust

Territory Air Service to fly two Grumman SA-16 Albatross amphibians on the Mariana–Caroline and Marshall Islands route in the Pacific South Seas after the previous operator, Transocean Airlines, went bankrupt. Flying the 642 miles from the old Pan Am Pacific Clipper base at Guam to Truk, 435 miles from Truk to Ponape, and 780 miles back to Guam, the two 15-seat "Clipper Ducks" or "Tuna Boats" flew the route plus numerous SAR flights in the area for eight years.

At the same time, Pan Am Albatrosses were supporting the US Air Force Eastern Test Range tracking station on Mahe in the Seychelles off the east coast of Africa. The amphibians had been on station since July 1963 when they were operated by the Philco-Ford Corp, with Pan Am taking over the contract in January 1965 and flying regular support flights from Mombasa until July 1971.

NORTH AMERICA

By the end of the 1960s, the last bastion of commercial big 'boat operations had moved to North America and the Caribbean. Based at Long Beach, California was Avalon Air Transport, later Catalina Air Lines Inc, which operated a shuttle service to nearby Catalina Island using a fleet of Grumman Goose amphibians. In 1957, they were joined by the former American Export Airlines transatlantic Sikorsky VS-44A *Excalibur*, which was converted to carry 47 passengers on the 50-mile San Pedro to Avalon Bay route. After 10 years of reliable service, the the 25-year-old flying

ABOVE For nearly 30 years, Avalon Air Transport, later Air Catalina, used Grumman Goose amphibians alongside the VS-44A flying from San Pedro Harbor, one of which is seen here taking off from Catalina Bay.

BELOW Ansett's Sandringham was sold to Antilles Air Boats in 1974 and renamed *Southern Cross*. It is seen here at its moorings at St Croix in the US Virgin Islands in 1977.

ABOVE Former American Export Airlines' Sikorsky VS-44A *Excalibur* was converted to a 47-seater by Avalon Air Transport in 1957 to fly a shuttle service between Long Beach, California and Catalina Island.

boat was sold to Antilles Air Boats, created by former American Export Airline's pilot Charles Blair in 1964, to join his fleet of Goose and Widgeon amphibians flying between San Juan, Puerto Rico, and the US Virgin Islands. In 1974 Blair, who was married to Hollywood actress Maureen O'Hara, added the two former Ansett Sandringhams to his growing operation, along with four 10-passenger Grumman Mallards. Two years later, Blair presented the veteran *Excalibur* to the Naval Aviation Museum at Pensacola, but following his fatal accident in a Goose in 1978, Antilles Air Boats closed and its operations were taken over by the Virgin Islands Seaplane Shuttle. The new airline took over the Mallard fleet, but the last of the world's commercial big 'boats were sold off to private collectors, and both have been preserved for future generations to enjoy.

The twin-engine 10-seat Grumman Mallard commercial transport amphibian, which first flew in April 1946, was virtually a scaled-up Goose. Due to its relatively high cost of $100,000 and the number of war-surplus aircraft that flooded the market in the late 1940s, it sold in small numbers mainly to large corporations as an executive transport. Ford, General Motors, Texaco, Shell, Twentieth Century Fox, and Christian Dior were all Mallard customers, although a few were also purchased by airlines such as BC Airlines of Canada, Japan's Nitto Airways, and Wein Consolidated in Alaska.

As the corporate amphibians were replaced by more sexy "biz-jets" in the 1960s, they were picked up by airlines around the world. The USA's oldest airline, Chalk's International, flying much the same route network since it started, from Watson Island, Miami to the Bahamas, began to replace its fleet of Goose and

Widgeon amphibians with Mallards. In 1979, four of these had their 600hp Pratt & Whitney Wasp piston engines replaced by 715shp Pratt & Whitney Canada PT6A turboprops built by Frakes Aviation. This enabled them to carry up to 17 passengers at a 200mph cruising speed. The Virgin Islands Seaplane Shuttle became the largest commercial Mallard operator with a mixed fleet of 12-piston and Turbo Mallards, while other Turbo Mallards found their way to Canada and Australia.

EUROPE

Grumman had the virtual monopoly of post-war commercial amphibian production; the Widgeon was built under license in France, although Italy and Britain continued to build the type in the early post-war period. In 1948 the Italian Piaggio company, which had built Dornier Wals in the 1930s, designed a neat twin pusher-engined gull-wing five-seat amphibian, the P136. Initially underpowered, it was re-engined with more powerful Piaggio-built 270hp Lycoming engines which gave it a top speed of nearly 200mph and a maximum range of 1,000 miles. A number of small air taxi operators ordered the P136L, including Dagens Nyheter in Sweden operating close to the Arctic Circle, Macao Air Transport, and Time Air and Eastern Provincial Airways in Canada. Two P136L-2s were operated by the Greek airline Olympic Airways for the almost exclusive use of its owner, Aristotle Onassis, and his family. One of these amphibians was to make world headlines in 1973 when SX-BDC crashed on take-off from Athens Airport, killing the pilot, Onassis's only son Alexander.

In Britain several air taxi operators had acquired former military Walrus biplane amphibians, but they proved to be

ABOVE In the 1980s, the Australian airline Air Whitsunday flew a Grumman Mallard from Mackay in Queensland on regular flights over the spectacular Great Barrier Reef.

BELOW One of Antilles Air Boats' large fleet of Grumman Mallard amphibians water-taxies to the seaplane terminal at St Croix past the ex-Ansett Sunderland.

ABOVE One of the last amphibians to be built in Europe was the Italian Piaggio P136L-2, one of which is seen here in Florida, where it was marketed as the Trecker Royal Gull 200.

OPPOSITE RIGHT The last airworthy British big boat was the ex-RAF/RNZAF civilized Short Sunderland V, brought back to Britain from the US Virgin Islands by Edward Hulton in 1982 after being sold by Antilles Air Boats.

uneconomical and soon disappeared from the civil register. A few that were used commercially with some success were three ex-Royal Navy amphibians used by United Whalers for whale spotting from factory ships in the Antarctic during the 1947 whaling season. However, Short Brothers had decided to produce a "baby" Solent to compete with the Grumman amphibians, and produced the Sealand, an attractive all-metal twin-engine amphibian seating a maximum of seven passengers, which first flew in January 1948.

Unfortunately, its career got off to a bad start when the second production aircraft crashed on a sales tour to Norway, killing all three crew. Its first customer, British West Indian Airways, canceled its order for three Sealands after unsatisfactory sea trials in the Caribbean.

After several modifications to improve its performance in the air and on the water, a number of Sealands were sold to corporations such as Shell, the Christian Missionary Alliance of New York, the East Bengal Transport Commission, and an executive version to a director of the Egyptian Khedivial Shipping Line, which featured hide upholstery for six passengers, air-conditioning, a built-in wine cabinet, and a bookcase. Only four were sold to airlines, two each to the Norwegian VLS at Bergen,

ABOVE Shorts' last flying boat design was the neat but underpowered amphibian, the Sealand, which was produced in small numbers in the 1950s but could not compete with the Grumman amphibians.

ABOVE LEFT In 1994, the veteran civilized Sunderland V built in 1944, the last airworthy example of its type, was sold to wealthy aircraft collector Kermit Weeks, and is kept in airworthy condition in Florida.

BOTTOM The owner of this former Ansett and Antilles Air Boats Sunderland, moored in the Pool of London in 1982, planned to use it for air cruises to exotic locations, but after damage in the Medway it was sold.

which operated a fleet of Republic Seabee amphibians, and the Yugoslav airline JAT, which operated an Adriatic coastal service with the Sealands.

After a production run of only 23, the Sealand line closed in November 1953 almost exactly 40 years to the day after the Short brothers Eustace, Horace, and Oswald flew their first seaplane. The Sealand was also Britain's last flying boat.

C-FTXI

The twenty-first century sees large flying boats being looked on as extinct prehistoric monsters. However, the big flying boat is alive and well. It continues to fill a niche in aviation that cannot be filled by any other type of aircraft. At the other end of the scale, thousands of private pilots in North America continue to fly floatplanes and single-engine amphibians for pleasure.

LEFT The giant 55-year old *Hawaii Mars*, seen here dropping a 12-ton water bomb during a fire-fighting sortie, is normally based at Sproat Lake on Vancouver Island but the FIFT boats often deploy to California during the forest fire season.

ABOVE Surplus Russian Navy "Mails" are being converted to firefighting Be-12P amphibians capable of scooping 1,500 gallons of water into their internal tanks.

CANADAIR CL-215

Firefighting and search and rescue amphibian with a crew of two to six was the first post-war commercial flying boat to be produced in quantity.

STATISTICS

Wingspan	98ft 10in	
Length	65ft	
Height	29ft 6in	
Weight	Empty 26,491lb	Loaded 43,500lb
Engines	Two 2,100hp Pratt & Whitney R-2800 radials	
Max speed	218mph	
Cruise speed	181mph	
Range	1,300 miles	
Payload	26 passengers; 6 tons of water/foam retardant	

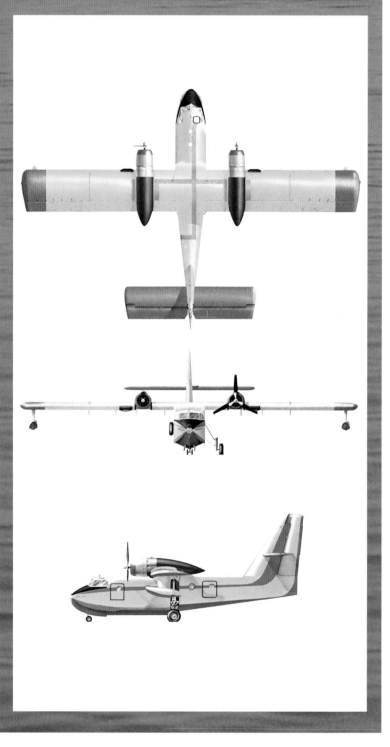

ABOVE The veteran turboprop Be-12 "Tchaika" amphibian remained in service with the Russian and Ukrainian navies at the end of the twentieth century, mainly in the **SAR** role.

These range from World War Two-vintage Piper Cubs on floats to the latest version of the four-seat Lake Turbo Buccaneer, more than 1,250 of which have been produced since 1950. Enthusiast warbird collectors keep more than a dozen ex-military Grumman Albatross amphibians airworthy, and in recent years these veterans have undertaken some epic long-distance flights. In 1993–94 former USAF HU-16C N888AC was flown around the world, while an ex-US Navy Albatross flew from the USA to Australia around the Pacific rim in 1995–96.

THE SURVIVORS

The Grumman amphibian soldiered on into the 1990s with at least two air forces, and the Greek Navy only relinquished the last of its ex-Norwegian HU-16B (ASW) Albatrosses when they were replaced by Lockheed P-3 Orions in 1998. A commercial cargo version was used by the Indonesian airline Pelita for offshore oil-support work until the mid-1990s.

Meanwhile, bush-flying air charter operators have made good use of seaplanes in remote regions of the world, particularly floatplane versions of the rugged range of short-take-off and landing (STOL) transport aircraft built by de Havilland, Canada. The single piston-engine seven-seat Beaver, the 10-seat Otter, and the twin turboprop-powered Twin Otter are still in common use in more than a dozen countries. Members of the Grumman family of twin-engine amphibians also soldier on in airline service, particularly on the west coast of Canada and the USA, and the islands of the Caribbean.

Peninsula Airways continues to use the veteran Goose in Alaska, as does the Canadian airline Trans-Provincial on scheduled flights from Prince Rupert Island, while a fleet of 15-passenger Turbo Mallards continues to be operated by America's oldest airline, Chalks, which was taken over by Pan Am, from Miami's Watson Island to the Bahamas. A surprise exhibit at the 1995 Paris Air Show at Le Bourget was a Turbo-Mallard shown by Frakes Aviation, which was proposing to re-start turbo-conversions of the dozen or more surviving piston-engine amphibians. The Albatross was briefly operated by Chalks but

ABOVE A former US Navy HU-16C Albatross amphibian fitted out as a luxury yacht was flown by John and Joyce Proctor across the Pacific to Lake Bora in Australia from Oregon, USA in 1995–96.

proved to be uneconomical as a commercial aircraft. Although a turboprop conversion, using Rolls-Royce Darts, was proposed, none are in airline service.

The Virgin Islands Seaplane Shuttle, based at San Juan, Puerto Rico, uses two piston-engine and one Turbo Mallard, survivors of Hurricane *Hugo*, which destroyed five of the airline's fleet of amphibians in September 1989.

Nevertheless, numerous environmental agencies have found the amphibian to be an invaluable asset for resource surveys and oceanographic research. Albatrosses are used by the Smithsonian Institution's Marine Systems Laboratory and the Seawings Laboratory in California, while an immaculate PBY-5A Catalina is operated by the international environmental campaign organization Greenpeace.

Never built in large numbers except during World War Two, the multi-engine flying boat has managed to carve out a niche for itself, fulfilling a whole range of very specific roles better than any other aircraft type.

ABOVE Small feeder airlines and charter operators use fleets of DH Canada floatplanes, such as these DHC Beavers, in North and South America, the Caribbean, and Australasia.

ABOVE RIGHT A Chalks International Airways 15-seat Grumman Turbo Mallard amphibian water-taxies away from its Watson Island terminal against the Miami skyline to begin a schedule to the Bahamas.

RIGHT The first and only US customer for the 28-passenger G.111 Albatross, shown at the 1982 Paris Air Show with a price-tag of $3.3 million, was Chalks International, for flights between Miami and Nassau.

BELOW RIGHT Long-time flying boat operator Air Whitsunday has operated a fleet of Beaver floatplanes, Lake Buccaneers, and a single Turbo Mallard for flying tourists out to Australia's Great Barrier Reef.

BELOW Many of the 1,000-plus single-engine Republic RC-3 Seabee amphibians built in the late 1940s are still active with private owners particularly in North, Central, and South America.

FIREFIGHTING

Search and rescue and, above all, aerial firefighting are the roles that have ensured the survival of the species. In a world that is only too conscious of losing its natural resources, catastrophic forest fires in North America, Southern Europe, Australasia, and Russia have accelerated the need for effective aerial water-bombers that can fight forest fires in remote and inaccessible regions.

The art of aerial water-bombing was developed after the end of World War Two when large numbers of military aircraft became surplus to requirements and new roles had to be found for them. Among these stocks being sold off at knock-down prices were US Navy Catalinas and the mighty Martin Mars. The former, mainly some of the 396 Canadair-built PBY-5A Canso amphibians, were fitted with water scoops which retracted into the hull. When the scoops were extended, the Canso was able to fill internal water tanks as it taxied on a lake or river at high speed. The water could then be dropped on a forest fire by opening "bomb" bay doors also built into the hull.

In 1960, the four surviving ex-US Navy Mars flying boats were acquired by Forest Industries Tankers Limited of Canada and modified for water-bombing. The firefighting Mars, still the world's largest flying boat, could pick up 6,000 gallons of water in 22 seconds (skimming the surface at 70mph) and make a drop from 150 to 250 feet every 15 minutes. Based at Sproat Lake, Vancouver Island, the fleet is set to serve on into the twenty-first century. In 1998, the 53-year-old boats *Philippine Mars* and *Hawaii Mars* were deployed for six months to Long Beach harbor, where they were in action against numerous fierce fires that plague southern California in the hot summer season. To date there is no replacement in sight for these veteran heavyweights.

While these surplus boats were being converted to water-bombers in the 1950s and 60s, it was the Canadian company, Canadair, that developed the first dedicated multi-engine firefighting flying boat in the 1970s, the CL-215. In Ontario Province alone, more than 1,000 fires a year were destroying millions of dollars' worth of timber, and in 1963 Canada's National Research Council issued a requirement for a dedicated

ABOVE The international environmental campaign group **Greenpeace** operates an immaculate **PBY-5A Catalina** with a fleet of helicopters and a hot-air balloon in support of its environmental research.

firefighting amphibian. Powered by two 2,100hp Pratt & Whitney R-2800 radial engines, it had a wingspan of 93 feet and was designed to scoop 1,200 gallons of water in 10 seconds skimming at approximately 82mph.

Deliveries of 124 production CL-215s began in June 1969 and finished in May 1990. Apart from five Canadian provinces, which purchased a total of 49 aircraft, firefighting CL-215s were also sold to the governments of France, Greece, Italy, Spain—the largest customer which eventually operated a total of 30—and Yugoslavia. The Royal Thai Navy operates two amphibians in the maritime patrol and SAR roles, while two more were purchased by a Venezuelan mining company as a 26-passenger transport operating from the River Orinoco. Second hand CL-215s have also been sold to Italy and Croatia.

However, the success of the rugged water-bomber has not disguised the fact that aerial firefighting is a dangerous business. The fires they target from 100 feet are often obscured by thick smoke fanned by strong winds and surrounded by rising heat eddies. Inevitably, more than a dozen aircraft and their crews have been lost while operating in these difficult environments, but the maneuverability and strength of the CL-215 has also saved many crews who would have perished had they been flying in many other types of aircraft.

LEFT The first dedicated firefighting flying boat was built by Canadair in the 1970s and more than 120 CL-215 amphibians had been sold to 10 different countries when production was phased out in 1990.

BOTTOM LEFT One of 20 Canadair CL-215 amphibious water-bombers delivered to the government of Quebec in the 1970s skimming across a lake scooping 1,200 gallons of water into its internal tanks.

In 1986, CL-215 customers were offered a turboprop retrofit to improve performance and extend the life cycle of these specialist amphibians. Some 20 CL-215Ts fitted with 2,380shp Pratt & Whitney PW123AF turboprops had been delivered by 1998, while a new upgraded version known as the CL-415 was launched by Canadair's new owner, Bombardier, in 1994.

BELOW The world's largest active flying boat, the Martin Mars, seen here at Long Beach, California with a Catalina under its wing, is one of two operated by Forest Industries Flying Tankers Ltd as water-bombers.

RECONNAISSANCE AND SEARCH AND RESCUE

However, Canadair was not the only manufacturer to carry on its traditional craft as a flying boat manufacturer. Having built a series of large four-engine maritime patrol Kawanishi flying boats in World War Two, and before that built Short Calcuttas under licence in the 1930s, the Japanese company Shin Maywa launched its high-tech PS-1 anti-submarine flying boat in 1968. Powered by four 3,060shp General Electric T64 turboprops and fitted with high-lift "blown" wing and tailplane flaps, the PS-1 could operate

in 10-foot waves and take off in only 260 feet of water. With a wingspan of 110 feet and carrying a crew of 10, the Shin Maywa flying boat, which weighed 32 tons, had a range of 1,500 miles and could be refueled from ships at sea.

After 22 PS-1s were built for the Japanese Maritime Self Defense Force (JMSDF) and six were lost mainly due to pilot error, production was switched to the US-1, an amphibious search and rescue variant. With more powerful engines and carrying an increased crew of 12, the US-1 patrols at 266mph and has a maximum range of 2,300 miles. Sixteen US-1As have been built

LEFT A Canadair CL-215 amphibian of the Spanish Air Force, the type's largest operator, dropping chemical foaming agents on a forest fire near Valencia.

BOTTOM RIGHT The rescue crew of a 71st Squadron Shin Maywa US-71A practice with the amphibian's motor-powered inflatable dinghy while the flying boat water-taxies in a moderate sea swell.

since it entered service with the JMSDF's 71st Air Rescue Squadron based at Iwakuni in 1980, and production is continuing at the rate of one per year.

Future US-1s will be substantially upgraded with even more powerful (4,000shp) turboprops, a fly-by-wire control system, glass cockpits, and the use of weight-reducing composite components. However the price tag for a twenty-first century US-1 will be a weighty $75 million per aircraft!

Japan's mainland neighbor, the People's Republic of China, surprised the aviation world when it announced in 1986 that it had designed and built a large maritime reconnaissance and SAR amphibian to replace its aging fleet of Soviet-built Be-6 flying boats. Powered by four 4,200shp Woijang turboprops, the Harbin PS-5's deep hull resembled the Shin Maywa US-1 but featured a glazed nose surrounding a large radome and twin tailfins. Fixed floats are mounted on the 118-foot span shoulder-mounted wing. However, the protracted development of the Harbin PS-5 has meant that only six had been produced for the Chinese People's Navy by 1999, one of which was converted to a water-bomber.

With its vast tracts of land crossed by few roads but numerous rivers, lakes, and inland waterways, China has a requirement for more than 500 six- to 30-seat amphibians over the next 20 years. In 1993, the Chengdu Asia Water Aircraft Company was formed to import, and later produce under license, up to 150 Lake Turbo 270 Renegade amphibians, which are the latest in a long line of single-piston engine Skimmers and Buccaneers produced by Lake Aircraft in Florida. A four-seat paramilitary development of the Renegade, the Seawolf has been adopted by a number of government agencies including those of Peru, Iraq, the Maldive Islands, and the US Florida Marine Patrol for various roles such as inland coastal and fisheries patrol, anti-smuggling, and a variety of other special operations.

However, the world's first twin turboprop powered amphibian, the Be-12 Seagull that entered service with the Soviet Navy in 1964, has outlived all other military flying boats of its era and still serves with Russian and Ukrainian naval units to this day. More than 200 of these versatile amphibians were built at Taganrog on the shores of the Sea of Asov between 1960 and 1975, serving in the maritime reconnaissance, photo-survey, Arctic support, submarine and warship co-operation, transport, search and rescue, and electronic warfare roles. Powered by two 4,190shp Ivchenko AI-20 turboprops, the Be-12 had a normal crew of five, a maximum speed of 378mph, and an endurance of up to 15 hours. At the height of the Cold War, the amphibian, given the NATO codename "Mail," was a familiar sight to NATO aircraft patrolling the Baltic Sea and during the frequent Arab–Israeli crises of the 1970s, Soviet-crewed Be-12s appeared in the eastern Mediterranean, while in the 1980s, Vietnamese "Mails" operated from Cam Rahn Bay, the old hunting ground of US Navy Marlin flying boats 20 years earlier.

BERIEVS AND DORNIERS

Since the end of the Cold War, Beriev has converted a number of surplus Be-12s into scientific research and ecological reconnaissance platforms, and water-bombers. Fires in Russia's Far Eastern provinces have been increasing in number and intensity during the 1990s and the country has a requirement for up to 100 water-bombers, but has no available budget. However, the Be-12 has proved to be a cost effective interim solution although less than a dozen aircraft have been converted to date. The Beriev Be-12P can scoop 1,500 gallons of water into three internal tanks in 15 seconds skimming at 75mph. Operating 60 miles from its base and five miles from available water, the amphibian can drop a total of 40 tons of water before refueling.

One of the last and best-kept Soviet secrets that was only revealed at the end of the Cold War was the Beriev A-40 Albatross, the world's most advanced and largest amphibian. With a wingspan of over 136 feet and a length of more than 143 feet, the A-40 was powered by two 24,000lb thrust D-30KPV turbofans plus two 6,500lb thrust R-60K booster jets used for

water take-offs. Its fully pressurized fuselage accommodated a crew of eight, and with a maximum speed of 500mph, the amphibian could carry 6.5 tons of ASW weapons over a range of 3,500 miles.

Beriev began designing the Be-12's successor for the Soviet Navy in 1982, and the first prototype of the long-range maritime reconnaissance, anti-submarine warfare, and minelaying A-40 flew in December 1986, with the Soviet Navy placing an order for 40 production aircraft in 1991. Unfortunately, as production of this remarkable aircraft began, the Soviet Union disintegrated and defense funds dried up. Only three A-40s were built, one of which was used for static testing. A projected version was the Be-42, an SAR amphibian with a crew of nine, comprehensive search/weather radar, two LPS-6 semi-rigid rescue boats, a rescue hoist, and a special loading hatch for up to 54 survivors or 21 stretchers. On board was a fully-equipped operating theater with a resuscitation unit and accommodation for extra paramedics. The Be-42 prototype was 90 percent complete when the program was canceled due to lack of funds. However, the technology used in the advanced Beriev amphibians has not been entirely lost as we shall see in the next chapter.

BELOW A Chinese People's Republic Navy Harbin PS-5 maritime reconnaissance, anti-submarine warfare, and SAR amphibian on its step during take-off from a coastal inlet on China's east coast.

TOP It is interesting to note that the advanced A-40 Mermaid ASW amphibian was subject to an evaluation by the UK Ministry of Defence as a possible replacement for the RAF's Nimrod maritime patrol aircraft, but nothing came of it.

LEFT Professor Claudius Dornier continued to champion the flying boat and was developing the Seastar amphibian design at the time of his death in April 1986.

At the 1983 Paris Air Show, Claudius Dornier came out of retirement to announce his latest design—the Seastar, a high-tech amphibious version of his first successful flying boat, the Wal. Built largely of composite materials, the 10-seat Seastar was powered by two 500shp Pratt & Whitney Canada PT6A turboprops in tandem, and featured the Dornier trademark sponsons in place of conventional wingtip floats. The first prototype made its maiden flight in August 1984 but was badly damaged while landing on Lake Constance a year later. In April 1986, Claudius Dornier died and the project was taken over by his two sons, but, following the flight of a second Seastar in October 1990, the venture faltered for lack of investment and the design was sold to a Malaysian group of companies two years later. Unfortunately, the economic crisis of the late 1990s hit the Far East badly and plans to produce the innovative Seastar in Malaysia came to nothing.

Lifelong flying boat devotee Georgii Beriev was a contemporary of Claudius Dornier, whose company is still involved in flying boat projects. In 1981 Dornier won a three-year contract from the Federal Ministry of Research and Technology to study a new amphibious flying boat design. As a research prototype the company converted a pre-war designed ex-Spanish Do 24 flying boat as a technology demonstrator. Three 1,125hp Pratt & Whitney PT6 turboprops replaced the original BMW piston engines and a radical new wing design and tricycle landing gear was fitted. The "new" Do 24TT first flew in April 1983 and successfully completed 85 hours of flight and sea trials over the next two years, but the project was not developed further.

However, with production of at least three big flying boats, a single-engine amphibian, and numerous floatplane versions of light aircraft set to continue well into the future, the breed looks more healthy than at any time over the final quarter of the twentieth century—and there is more to come.

TOP Claudius Dornier's last flying boat design was the composite Seastar, which first flew in August 1984, but his death and the loss of the prototype in an accident at Lake Constance retarded its development.

RIGHT The world's most sophisticated military amphibian, the jet-powered Beriev A-40 Albatross was designed in the dying years of the Soviet Union, but there was no money for its production.

PHOENIX RISING

At the time of writing, heavier-than-air flight is less than a hundred years old, and the flying boat even younger. Although the flying boat reached its peak in the 1930s and 1940s and ever since has seemed to be in a steady decline, the facts show that this decline may have been arrested.

LEFT The first new Russian multi-engine design to fly since the end of the Cold War was Beriev's advanced jet-powered amphibious flying boat. The Be-200 made its maiden flight from Irkutsk in September 1998.

ABOVE Some of the features of the Centaur include its folding wing for ease of mooring, its slender hydrodynamic hull, and the combined sponsons and loading platform.

BERIEV BE-200

Jet powered firefighting and commercial transport amphibian with a crew of two is the latest of a long line of Beriev flying boats destined to go into service with Russian environmental agencies in 2000.

STATISTICS

Wingspan	107ft 4in	
Length	105ft	
Height	29ft 3in	
Weight	Empty 82,000lb	Loaded 108,000lb
Engines	Two 16,550lb st Zaporozhsky D-436Tp turbofans	
Max speed	445mph	
Cruise speed	380mph	
Range	2,240 miles	
Payload	72 passengers; 12 tons of water/foam retardant	

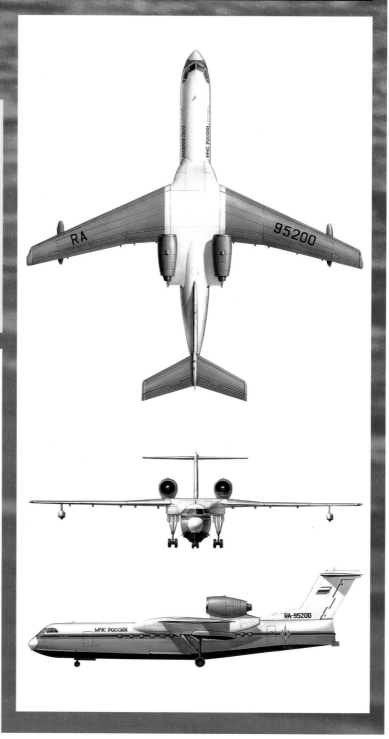

INTO THE NEXT MILLENNIUM

At the end of the twentieth century there were more than 4,500 active 4–8-seat seaplanes, at least 1,000 of which were used commercially. There are more than 60 seaplane flying schools in North America alone. In addition to these, which are mainly single-engine floatplanes, there are nearly 300 multi-engine flying boats in service which bodes well for the breed, if we bear in mind that in the late 1930s, regarded as the golden age of the flying boat, there were fewer than 500 multi-engine 'boats in military and commercial worldwide operation.

The Japanese manufacturer Shin Maywa will continue to produce at least one high-tech US-1A SAR amphibian for the Japanese Maritime Self-Defense Force over the next five years, while Canadair sees production of its CL-415 firefighter, the first of which was delivered in 1995, as being slow but steady over the next two decades. Powered by two 2,380shp Pratt & Whitney Canada PW123AF turboprops, the CL-415 fitted with an

LEFT The shape of the twenty-first century flying boat, a Canadair CL-415 amphibian firefighter, a turboprop development of the piston-engine CL-215. More than 125 were produced in the 1970s and 1980s.

RIGHT The Canadair CL-415 turboprop-powered firefighter dropping a six-and-a-half-ton water-bomb through its computer-controlled four-door drop system which optimizes drop patterns.

BELOW RIGHT One of 12 Canadair CL-415 amphibian water-bombers replacing 15 piston-engine CL-215s with France's Sécurité Civile, seen skimming over a lake scooping 1,350 gallons of water in 12 seconds.

electronic flight instrument system and fully powered flight controls, can drop a 1,620-gallon load, or six-and-a-half tons of water or fire retardants from modified tanks using its computer-controlled four-compartment drop system. On an average firefighting mission, six miles from water source to site of fire, the CL-415 can complete nine drops per hour delivering 14,500 gallons of water. Fifty aircraft plus five options had been ordered by 1999.

The firefighter is being marketed with Canadair's integrated fire management system, a computer-based information management system which predicts fire danger, occurence, and behavior, and collates information from fire surveillance sources be they aerial patrols, observers in lookout towers, or by remote TV and infra-red systems. Even a two-hour delay between the start of a fire and its detection can be critical in preventing widespread devastation.

Some 20 percent of its future sales is expected to come from the military sector. Maritime surveillance, search and rescue, and special operations are roles ideally suited to the turboprop amphibian. The CL-415M will have underwing hardpoints and pylons for long-range fuel tanks, stores, and other weapons payload. The turboprop's extra power and reverse pitch propellers shorten the take-off distance to 2,670 feet and the landing run to 2,180 feet on water, and the CL-415 is able to operate for 96 percent of the time in the Mediterranean and 80 percent of the time in the Atlantic. The turboprop Canadair is also an efficient people and cargo-mover—carrying 35 passengers or 6,600lb of

freight over a range of more than 1,000 miles with full fuel reserves. It is designed to quickly climb to an economic cruising height to give the CL-415 a maximum cruising speed of 235mph, a performance which is competitive with many contemporary landplanes around today.

THE RUSSIAN CHALLENGE

Canadair's faith in the long-term future of the flying boat has been shared by post-Communist Russia, which has produced a number of innovative amphibian designs. New companies were set up by designers leaving the old monolithic Soviet design bureaus in the early 1990s hoping that private enterprise would finance their projects. This, unfortunately, has proved to be a false hope in many instances.

ROS-Aeroprogress is one such company. Established in 1990, its investors included various Yak and Myasishchyev production plants whose government contracts had all but dried up, to produce a series of general aviation types. The company has designed two waterborne aircraft to date, the T-130 Fregat, a twin turboprop tandem-powered 15-passenger amphibian that bears more than a passing resemblance to the Claudius Dornier Seastar, and the T-1433 Flamingo, a single piston-engine five-seat multi-role amphibian that could be mistaken for a Lake Renegade. Although work on a Fregat prototype was begun, lack of finances prevented its completion, while the Flamingo remains on the drawing board. However, an amphibious floatplane version of its successful T-101 Grach, a single-turboprop 10-passenger utility transport in the Beaver catagory, has flown and is in production.

Even the mighty Molniya Design Bureau which produced the Soviet Union's Buran space shuttle orbiter (which was never used), has begun work on a six-seat gull-winged light multi-role amphibian powered by two 450hp pusher piston engines inspired by the Piaggio P136L.

One of the most promising designs has come from Aviaspetstrans, a consortium formed in 1989 by a group of research, engineering, and prospecting organizations, again with production backing from the Myasishchyev production plant, to promote air transport in Siberia and the Far East and polar regions of Russia.

The Yamal is a 70-foot wingspan amphibian capable of carrying a maximum of 18 passengers, cargo, or scientific instrumentation at a speed of 250mph over a maximum range of 1,500 miles. Its novel engine layout comprises two 1,300shp TVD turboprops mounted in the rear cabin geared to drive a single propeller behind the tail. This gives the Yamal twin-engine power with excellent directional stability on the water and with no asymmetric problems in the event of an engine failure on take-off. Designed for ease of maintenance, autonomous operation in regions with minimum air transport infrastructure, and operating in extreme climatic conditions, it can take off and land on stretches of lakes, rivers, or reservoirs of less than 1,500 feet, or on moderate seas. It has underwing pylons for scientific monitoring equipment, cameras, or thermal imaging systems.

Myasishchyev constructed a full-scale mock-up of the Yamal, which was first displayed at the 1992 Mosaeroshow, and work on a prototype was commenced but, with Russia's economy entering a downward spiral in the late 1990s, it is difficult to predict when, or even if, the Yamal will make its first flight.

BERIEV FIGHTS BACK

One Russian company that has never lost faith in the flying boat is also one of the world's most experienced designers of marine aircraft. The Beriev Design Bureau, located on the shores of the Sea of Asov, has been continuously producing flying boats for almost 70 years and has had a monopoly of marine aircraft in Russia since 1948. After the disappointment of the magnificent A-40 Albatross and the virtual halt of military contracts, Beriev's chief general designer, Gennari Panatov, went back to basics. In 1990 he formed the Taganrog Aviation Scientific Technical Complex company to design, manufacture, and market several new commercial flying boat designs, the first of which was the innovative Be-103.

A light six-seat multi-role amphibian powered by two 150hp M-17 piston engines mounted on lateral pylons behind the passenger cabin, the Be-103 is also designed to operate in any environment. An unusual feature is its low-mounted almost delta wing which also acts as sponsons. There are no traditional wing floats. Constructed largely of advanced composite and honeycomb materials, access to the cabin is through two large upward-hinged

doors in the roof which can be used to load bulky cargo or two stretchers. With a maximum cruising speed of 170mph and a range of 500 miles, the Be-103 first flew in 1997. Although the first prototype crashed a year later, through no design fault, a second Be-103 has since flown and the type is now in production.

Another Beriev project was the Be-112, a twin turboprop-powered multi-role amphibian in the same class as the Yamal to which it was similar in appearance and design. It has not progressed beyond the drawing board.

On September 24, 1998 the first flight of the Be-200, a potent competitor to Canadair's pre-eminence in the production of firefighting amphibians, took place at Irkutsk in Siberia. The Beriev Design Bureau had already begun developing a three-quarter-scale commercial version of its A-40 jet-powered maritime reconnaissance amphibian in the 1980s. Four versions of the fully pressurized Be-200 amphibian were planned, a 74-seat passenger

OPPOSITE The demanding and hazardous environment in which modern aerial firefighters operate can be seen as this Sécurité Civile CL-415 bombs a forest fire in a mountainous region of the south of France.

TOP Beriev's first post-Cold War commercial design was the Be-103, an innovative six-seat multi-purpose amphibian built largely of advanced composite materials and powered by two piston engines.

LEFT Having no wingtip floats, the Be-103's low-mounted delta-type wing-in-ground effect configuration acts both as sponsons and as a loading platform for passengers or cargo.

version, an eight-ton cargo version, a coastal patrol/search and rescue (SAR) version, and, most importantly, a firefighting water-bomber. However, the Be-200, which has the same supercritical wing design with leading-edge slats and speed brakes, "T" tail configuration, and engines mounted above the wings as the A-40, will be in a class of its own as a water-bomber. It will be able to scoop 12 tons of water into its eight internal tanks in 12 seconds over four-foot high waves, and drop 360 tons of water or fire retardants before refuelling if the fire zone is within six miles of a suitable water source. The amphibian can land or take off in a minimum of six feet depth of water and sea state three. The Be-200's integrated logistics support system, the ARIA-2000 jointly developed by the Russian Aviation Equipment Institute and the US company Allied Signals, will enable its two-man crew to compute the speed and distance required to fill its water tanks, and the speed, distance, and height down to 150 feet to make the most effective use of its 12-ton water "bomb" over a forest fire.

Powered by two 16,550lb thrust Zaporozhsky D-436TP turbofans, the 107.5-foot wingspan, 37-ton amphibian has a maximum speed of 445 mph, a maximum range of 2,400 miles, and is designed for western BMW–Rolls-Royce BR-715 or Allison-2000 turbofans to be installed. Although the first Be-200 was completed in September 1998, it was another year before sufficient funds were available for it to make its maiden flight.

LEFT The Beriev Be-200 amphibian's design benefits from the aerodynamic and hydrodynamic research that went into the development of its predecessor the A-40 Albatross maritime reconnaissance flying boat.

TOP Designed as a firefighter, the Be-200 has water scoops and four doors built into its hull for scooping and dropping 12 tons of water or fire retardants in three seconds.

NEW HORIZONS

Meanwhile, Shin Maywa in conjuction with the Society of Japanese Aerospace Companies has continued to carry out long-term studies into the possibility of developing new transport systems using amphibious aircraft. The ultimate goal of this ambitious project is to open routes to isolated islands and regional cities off the major air routes and where the construction of conventional airports would be difficult and prohibitively expensive.

The Japanese Agency of Industrial Science and Technology has been carrying out an assessment to determine the social impact of implementing such systems, while Shin Maywa has produced a number of new flying boat projects which would become an integral part of such a system. Four of these concepts are a 30 to 50-passenger jet-powered amphibious feeder-liner, 250-seat and 400-seat amphibians powered by four turbofans, and, lastly, a giant 1,200-seat long-haul commercial flying boat.

The most advanced, and possibly the most practical, of these projects is the Shin Maywa SS-X amphibious feeder-liner, which has reached the point where wind-tunnel testing has begun and detailed specification released. These are for an STOL amphibian with a maximum take-off weight of 17.5 tons and carrying a crew and 40 passengers at a cruising speed of 350mph over a range of

It was the first new multi-engine aircraft to fly in Russia since the end of the Cold War! Russia has a requirement for at least 100 modern firefighting aircraft over the next five years, and its Ministry of Emergency Situations became the Be-200's first customer when it ordered seven firefighting versions with limited accommodation for up to 26 firefighters or rescue personnel.

Russia's Federal Forestry Service has an option for 50 amphibians. Production of the Be-200 will be handled by the Irkutsk Aviation Industrial Association which previously produced large numbers of MiG-27 and Su-30 Cold War jet fighters. The exciting Be-200 is set to become a serious long-term competitor to the Canadair CL-415 and thus stimulate interest in big flying boats for the forseeable future.

OPPOSITE CENTER The two 16,550lb thrust D-436TP turbofan engines that power the Be-200 are mounted high above the wings to avoid spray ingestion during water take-offs and landings.

TOP The Beriev Be-200 has non-retractable wingtip floats for easy maintenance, weight, and cost savings.

RIGHT Russia's Ministry of Emergency Situations, which responds to natural disasters in remote regions, is the lead customer for Beriev's advanced and versatile Be-200 amphibian.

500 miles. Powered by two advanced turbofans of some 8,000lb thrust, the engines would be positioned high and forward of the wing that utilizes upper surface blowing flaps on the trailing edge, spoilers, and high-lift leading-edge slats. The tailplane, similar to that of the Be-200, is "T"-mounted to be clear of the jet exhaust and water spray while the stabilizing wing floats would be non-retractable for simplicity as well as to save cost and weight.

Another ambitious flying boat project is in the same league as the giant Japanese 1,200-seater. The Hydro 2000 designed by Frenchman Maurice Goutille will have a wingspan of 360 feet, a length of 350 feet, and will weigh 360 tons! Inspired by the projected Beriev and Dornier flying boat giants of 30 years ago, Goutille is convinced that modern advanced engine technology can turn such a project into reality. Designed to carry up to 500 tons of cargo for more than 5,000 miles cruising at 500mph, it would be powered by six 110,000lb thrust General Electric turbofans mounted on pylons above the wing and constructed of

ABOVE An artist's impression of Shin Maywa's tubofan-powered SS-X 40-passenger amphibious feeder-liner concept.

RIGHT This Beriev project for a giant 1,200-passenger flying boat has inspired the French Hydro 2000, a 350-ton cargo-carrier, being developed to carry Ariane rocket boosters from France to French Guyana, Africa.

LEFT Ross Aircraft has built a one-fifth scale concept model of its projected 10-seat amphibian to be developed from the highly-successful Britten-Norman Islander landplane.

BELOW The Warrior Centaur is an advanced all-composite six-seat amphibious flying boat aimed at replacing up to 1,000 aging commercially-operated floatplanes.

carbon composite materials and titanium to save weight and resist seawater corrosion.

Wind-tunnel testing of the design has already been carried out by the French aeronautical research organisation ONERA, and Goutille is negotiating with Canadair, Beriev, Lockheed Martin, and other potentially interested parties to cooperate in the development of the Hydro 2000 which will cost $12 million. Production of the flying boats, each of which is estimated to cost $400 million, will be at Port Autonome in Normandy, and they will fly from a supertanker harbor at Cap d'Antifer near Le Havre. Goutille plans to use the boats to fly the launch stages of France's new Ariane 5 space rocket from its assembly plant in southwest France to the European Space Centre in Kourou, French Guiana.

A practical and more cost-effective project was announced in 1995 by a British company. The Ross Aircraft Company has been developing a low-cost twin-engine amphibian based on the successful 10-seat Britten-Norman Islander, and has flown a one-fifth scale proof-of-concept model. Designed by David Thurston, who was responsible for the Lake Buccaneer's predecessor, the Skimmer, and had worked on several Grumman amphibians including the Mallard, the Ross amphibian will be powered by two 350hp Lycoming T10 piston engines fitted to a modified 53-foot span Islander/Defender 4000 wing and feature a retractable tail-wheel undercarriage. The 10-seat amphibian would cruise at 160mph and carry a full payload over a range of 1,000 miles. By choosing a proven airframe (more than 1,300

Islander/Defenders had been produced by the end of 1998), the Ross would have an extensive worldwide customer base and maintenance support network. However, the amphibian is only one part of a package being offered which would include the training of commercial seaplane pilots and the establishment of a commercial seaplane operating infrastructure comprising offset global positioning system alighting aids, remote sea state and wind direction measurement, low-environmental impact refueling systems, docking ramps, and handling terminals. This innovative approach, allied to an economical aircraft based on established commercial success, could see the re-establishment of flying boat manufacture in Britain for the first time for nearly 50 years.

A WARRIOR OF THE WAVES

Another British project takes a very different view of the future of the flying boat. Warrior (Aero-Marine) Ltd has designed a radical advanced technology amphibian to replace many of the 4,500 four to eight-seat seaplanes currently active. Many of these single-engine flying boats such as the Seabee and Buccaneer are more than 30 years old, while some floatplane versions of landplanes such as the Beaver and Otter are even older. Even more modern types such as the Cessna 180 and 206, which have reduced performances when fitted with floats, are no longer in production.

The Warrior Centaur high-tech single-engine six-seat amphibian has a new low-drag hull and high-lift aerodynamic wing constructed of carbon, glass, and Kevlar fibers. Although construction of the Claudius Dornier Seastar used largely composite materials, it had problems with the manufacture of certain components, but technology has moved on in leaps and bounds and this has enabled Warrior to use them with complete confidence. The slender, corrosion-free, low-maintenance hull gives the Centaur excellent sea-handling qualities and enables it to handle waves up to four feet in height, twice the height at which most single-engine seaplanes can operate.

Powered by a 300hp Lycoming IO-540 piston engine, the Centaur can fly 1,200 miles cruising at 150mph. Ease of loading on land or water is facilitated by the use of upward-hinged doors and the loading platform provided by the broad stub-wing sponsons, which also house the main-wheels of the tricycle undercarriage. Many waterside facilities that are too small to moor conventional seaplanes are accessible to the Centaur by virtue of its folding wing mechanism. With wings folded the Centaur takes up no more space than a 12-meter yacht. A larger 12 to 14-seat variant of the Centaur powered by a 600shp Pratt & Whitney Canada PT6A turboprop is on the drawing board.

Both Ross and Warrior are attempting to establish production of their projects in the United Kingdom, but according to past precedents they may join countless other innovative and practical British aviation projects overseas.

.Most of the world's seaplane population operates in North America and at least one American company is aiming at the same market as the Warrior Centaur. The Nauticair 400 amphibian, designed by a former Grumman engineer, Roy LoPresti, is another high-tech high performance project looking for investment. The six-passenger flying boat powered by a single 3,650lb thrust Allied Signal Garratt TFE731 turbofan has a maximum cruising

ABOVE The Centaur is designed to provide performance, handling, and economy competitive with contemporary similar-sized landplanes plus the advantage of being amphibious and having a corrosion-free structure.

BELOW A twin-engine nine-seat Nauticair 450 is powered by two 2,300lb thrust Williams/Rolls-Royce FJ44-2 turbofans and is aimed at the military.

speed of 515mph with a maximum range of 1,400 miles, and features a novel shoulder-mounted forward-swept wing and "T" tailplane. The sponsored tunneled hull minimizes drag at high speed, creating a wing-assisted hull-lifter. A twin-engine, nine-seat Nauticair 450, powered by two 2,300 lb thrust Williams/Rolls-Royce FJ44-2 turbofans is also being developed for the military.

At a predicted price of $3 million, the Nauticair Corporation based in Florida needs some $5 million to develop its advanced concept into reality.

FROM MiGS TO MONSTERS

Two other Russian projects use wing-in-ground effect (WIG) which was fully developed for a series of huge Ekranoplans designed by the Soviets in the 1960s. Part aircraft, part ship, the Ekranoplan or Wingship skims the water surface on a strip of compressed air "flying" no higher than 100 feet. In the 1970s and 1980s, the Soviet Navy operated a small fleet of 540-ton KM Ekranoplans with a wingspan of 131 feet, powered by 10 jet engines at speeds over 300mph, and able to carry some 500 troops! They were christened the "Caspian Sea Monsters."

In 1993 the once-powerful MiG Design Bureau which was responsible for the Korean War MiG-15 and the world's most prolific jet fighter, the MiG-21, designed a small four-seat amphibian, the TA-4, which could travel over any surface using an air-cushion landing system at speeds of up to 160mph. The TA-4 amphibian was never built.

More successful was the seven-passenger Aero-RIK designed by a team led by the Sokel production plant which produced the

ABOVE RIGHT The projected US Nauticair 400 uses a wing-assisted hull-lifter concept to give the six-passenger jet-powered amphibian unprecedented hydrodynamic stability.

RIGHT Wing-in-ground effect, used by giant Soviet Navy Ekranoplans known as "Caspian Sea Monsters," is being used in a number of advanced amphibious aircraft developments.

MiG-29 and MiG-31 fighters. It is another multi-role amphibian designed to operate over any surface with an 850shp Pratt & Whitney Canada PT6A turboprop for propulsion plus a 250shp TVA turboprop to provide the cushion effect. With a maximum speed of 200mph and a range of 500 miles, the Aero-RIK first "flew" in 1995 and limited production was reported to be underway in 1998.

A British design company, AVPRO Ltd, has produced a multi-role wing-assisted hull-lifter concept for the Royal Navy using a similar system to that of the Nauticair 400 and with a similar performance. The two to four-seat Marauder flying boat would be powered by two advanced turbofans fitted above the delta wing for low radar signature, and could be used as an airborne early warning platform, in the close air support and cruise missile launching roles, or for inserting small teams of special forces on hostile beaches and inland waterways. They would take off and land on water and could be launched from assault carriers lying offshore or from conventional shipping harbors.

OPPOSITE The US Marine Corps has shown interest in the stealthy jet-powered Marauder flying boat constructed with advanced composites for Special Operations (SO) and Combat Search And Rescue (CSAR).

The facts are that 70 percent of the world's surface is covered with water and that 80 percent of the world's economic activity on land takes place within 150 miles of the sea. Most of the world's capital cities are situated on the coast or on the banks of a river, while water runways cannot be destroyed by natural disasters or bombs. It is clear that there will always be a demand for the flying boat as long as man uses aircraft for private, commercial, or military purposes. In spite of earlier predictions, wings on water are here to stay.

ABOVE The AVPRO Marauder is another advanced wing-assisted hull-lifter designed for the Royal Navy to fulfill a number of specialized combat roles such as Close Air Support (CAS), and Airborne Early Warning (AEW).